The Seer's Guide to Symbolism

SIMILITUDES, METAPHORS, AND SYMBOLISM

Fred Raynaud

Book 4, The Seer Series
CELI Publication

Copyright © 2014 by Fred L. Raynaud.

All rights reserved. This book is protected by the copyright laws of the United States of America. This book may not be copied or reprinted for commercial gain or profit. The use of short quotations or occasional page copying for personal or group study is permitted and encouraged. Permission will be granted upon request. Unless otherwise identified, Scripture quotations taken from the New King James Version. Scripture taken from the New King James Version®. Copyright © 1982 by Thomas Nelson, Inc. Used by permission. All rights reserved. Emphasis within Scripture quotations are the author's own. Please note that the author capitalizes certain pronouns in Scripture that refer to the Father, Son, and Holy Spirit, and may differ from some authors and publishers' styles. Take note that the name satan and related names are not capitalized. The author chooses not to acknowledge him, even to the point of violating grammatical rules.

Fred Raynaud/The Seer's Guide to Symbolism
www.Seersgift.com

Book Layout ©2014 BookDesignTemplates.com
"Original and modified cover art by NaCDS and CoverDesignStudio.com"
Ordering Information:
Quantity sales. Special discounts are available on quantity purchases by corporations, associations, and others. For details, contact the "Special Sales Department" at our website.

The Seer's Guide to Symbolism/Fred Raynaud. —1st ed.
ISBN 978-0-9905959-0-8

Contents

Acknowledgement 7
Preface 9
Similitudes, Metaphors, & Symbolism 11
A 17
    Angels 17
    Animals 20
    Aroma 22
    Art 24
    Authority Figures 24
B 29
    Birth, Pregnancy, Babies, and Children 29
    Beverages, Drinking 31
    Birds 33
    Blood 35
    Body Parts 36
    Books, Scrolls, Letters, Writing 40
    Being Bound 42
    Bugs, Insects 43
    Buildings & Houses 43
C 45
    Celebration 45
    Cleaning & Cleaning Agents 45
    Colors 46
    Communication 48

- Confinement 48
- Construction, Building Something 49
- Containers (all kinds) 49
- Cooking 51
- Covering and Mantles 53
- Crime 53
- Crushed, Carried, Trapped, Stuck, Smothered 54

D 57
- Digging 57
- Direction 58
- Doors, Gates, Windows 58

E-F 63
- Education 63
- Emotions, Feelings, Reactions 64
- Farming, Planting, Plowing, Harvest 64
- Finance and Provision 65
- Fire 66
- Fish and Fishing 67
- Flying 68
- Food 69

G 71
- Garments and Clothing 71
- Gems, Jewels, Jewelry 74
- Geographic, Nations, and Cities 74
- Glory of God 75

H-K 79

Hell 79

Homelessness 79

Hygiene 80

Intersession, Watching 81

Keys 81

L 85

Ladders, Steps, and Stairs 85

Land, Soil, Deserts, Valleys 87

Light, Electricity, Lightning 89

M 93

Medical, Sickness, Healing 93

Metal 94

Mirrors, Pictures 95

Music and Worship 96

N 99

Numbers 99

O-P 109

Occult and Witchcraft 109

Oil 110

Plant Life 110

Q-R 117

Roads, Trails & Potholes 117

Rocks, Walls 118

Royalty 118

Running 119

S 121

    Seas, Lakes, Rivers, and Streams 121

    Seasons..125

    Sight, Eyes, and Lens 126

    Signs, Banners, and Billboards..127

    Sounds..128

    Space 130

    Speaking...130

    Sports & Games...131

    Stage, Platforms 135

T-Z..137

    Tickets 137

    Time..139

    Tools 139

    Transportation...142

    Trees 145

Bibliography...155

About the Author 157

To
Two of the strongest women I know
Jean Barrett
&
Sally Wizdo

Acknowledgement

There are several people I would like to acknowledge in the preparation of this book. Foremost I want to thank my wife Jan for putting up with my crazy schedule and supporting me while I got up in wee hours of the morning to take on this task.

Of course no writing effort would be complete without the diligence of a good Godly copyeditor, and Christy Jones, in spite of her tight schedule raising kids and preparing for various triathlons, heeded that call and helped me to hone my writing and stay focused on the subject at hand; thank you Christy, your work was a true blessing! Then there is my sister Jean, whose eye for detail caught all that we missed. Her attention to detail is incredible! Not too bad for a *very* bust grandmother! Love you Jean. Finely I would also like to thank my dear friend Leo Griego, for reading my early drafts and giving invaluable feedback and support.

Preface

*"I have also spoken by the prophets,
And have multiplied visions;
I have given symbols through the witness
of the prophets"*

- Hosea 12:10

This book is the fourth book in the Seer Series. In volume one we explored the concept of the Seer gift and briefly looked at the language of visions and dreams. Book 2 examined how the seer gift operates while ministering to the sick and hurting. Book three we looked at the seer gift and its relationship to prophecy and the office of the Seer Prophet. In this volume, we will look at symbolism and its relationship to the language of visions and dreams.

The ministry of the prophetic to the body of Christ has always been a passion of mine, partially due to my own personal gifting from God, but more so, to the impact it can have in the life of the believer. Visions and dreams are a big part of that gifting. This book is simple a guide for you to ponder as you pray about the symbols and metaphors God uses when speaking to you.

I pray that this book blesses you and you are encouraged to fulfill your destiny and call upon your life! May God richly bless you and pour out the spirit of revelation, grace, and truth upon your life. May you blossom into an incredible host of God's presence and may your hearts be filled with understanding and most of all... LOVE.

Enjoy...

Fred Raynaud

CHAPTER 1

Similitudes, Metaphors, & Symbolism

"As I walked through a great wilderness I came to a certain place where there was a Den, and I laid myself down in that place to sleep: and as I slept I dreamed a dream. I dreamed; and I thought that I saw in my dream a man standing with his face turned away from his own house. He was clothed in rags, a book was in his hand, and a great burden was on his back. Then I saw him open the book and read; and as he read, he wept and cried out, 'What shall I do?'."

— John Bunyan, The Pilgrim's Progress

This part of the book is devoted to the symbolism that the Holy Spirit uses to speak to us in dreams and visions. I wrote this section as a reference tool. I encourage you to return to this section of the book as many times as needed and ponder the various ways the Lord speaks to our hearts.

When I first started thinking about this chapter, I was drawn to that incredible pilgrim and warrior in the faith, John Bunyan. He is best remembered for his book "*The Pilgrims Progress*" which he says, was "*Delivered under the similitude of a DREAM.*" He wrote it from a prison cell almost three hundred fifty years ago (1678). John Bunyan's dream story has become the most famous allegory in English literature. Second only to the Bible, more people than any other religious book in history have read it. It has been translated into more languages than any other book in the English tongue.

In the book of Hosea we read:

> "*I have also spoken by the prophets, and I have multi-plied visions, and used similitudes, by the ministry of the prophets*"

> — Hosea 12:10, KJV

The Hebrew word for "similitude" in this verse is "dama" meaning to liken, to compare, to imagine, think, a symbol, or similitude. To that definition, I would include the words, metaphor, allegory, simile, and parable. As you can see from this book series, the Lord loves to speak through stories. His language is so broad and wide it defies our linier mindset. In this chapter, let's explore the language of similitudes and give examples on the various ways the Lord uses symbolism and metaphor to speak into our lives.

The following examples are general guideline for possible interpretation of visions and dreams and are in no way definitive. **Your number one source for interpretation is the Holy Spirit and the Word of God.** These insights simply come from the commonality found by many in the body of Christ as well as my own personal experience. *They are here to stimulate your thinking and cause you to ponder as you explore the depth of the language of God. Remember, everything is about context. The context of your of your dream or vision will help define its meaning and application.*

This is **not** a complete glossary of pectoral symbolism. I have simply chosen a few for the purpose of illustration. For those who want a more in depth look, James Goll's "Dream Language" is a great place to start. Another great resource is the ministry of John Paul Jackson and his class on "The Art of Hearing God." It is designed to train students to hear the voice of the Lord and to develop greater intimacy with Jesus Christ.

(http://www.streamsministries.com).

Moving in dreams and visions is available to every believer in some degree or another. While not everyone is called to the ministry of the seer-prophet, **all** can move to some extent in this realm.

In this book, I have tried to show the value of metaphor and teach you how God uses the language of visions and dreams to speak to you. I want to encourage you to learn to think metaphorically. Consider the way God speaks. Much of the Old Testament is given to us veiled in allegory, shadows, types, and metaphor. From Genesis to Revelation we see the fundamental truths of the Gospel and the face of Jesus woven throughout the Scriptures like nuggets of revelation tucked away in the melody of the Word.

The main reason people miss interpretations is by thinking in literal rather than metaphorical terms. God uses symbolism that is familiar to your life. God knows every aspect of your life. He often speaks utilizing your life experiences and the things that define you. He knows your life, your makeup, which you are, and what you do. He knows your passions, and interests, He is interested in you. If you are a mechanic, God may speak to you along those lines. If you are a Chef, God may show you culinary symbols. Jesus spoke to the people of His day in parables that they could relate. As an agrarian society that worked the land and fished in the Sea of Galilee, they understood when Jesus spoke of tilling the soil and casting out nets for a catch.

God may show you the same type of symbols and their meaning and be very consistent in their use, interpretation, and application. For instance, in the Word of God a lamb is a common symbol that has a consistent thread of meaning throughout Scripture. Whenever certain symbols manifest pictorially to you, it will become obvious what they mean.

On the other hand, God does not want us to turn His creative voice into a formula. His desire is to stretch us and cause us to dig for truth through fellowship with Him. He wants us to be constantly dependent upon Him and His Word. As soon as we think we have it down pat, He will show us a symbol that we thought we knew, and suddenly it make no sense at all. The Lord does this to keep our dependency on Him. Always seek Him and His Word to search out the meaning of His speech. John Paul Jackson put it this way regarding visionary interpretation:

> *"The closer we can maintain our intimacy with the Holy Spirit, the better we can begin to hear His voice in understanding what He is speaking to us. We can learn all the mechanics and they are immensely helpful, but after that we must depend upon His voice to lead us."*

Follow Daniel's lead. Daniel knew that *"Interpretations belong to God"* and He sought the Lord through prayer and the Lord revealed the meaning of the dream (Daniel

2). In the end, it is hearing His voice that brings the revelation.

Symbolism found in visions and dreams are often similar, however, the interpretation may be quite different. Often visions operate through the gifts of *"the word of knowledge," "discerning of spirits,"* or *"prophecy"* and the interpretation and application may come quickly, as God speaks to your heart regarding the matter. Dreams on the other hand may need more digging and often revolve around your life destiny, mission, life, and God's desire for you personally. I will try to bring this to light as we discuss similitudes.

As you learn the metaphorical language of the Holy Spirit, your ability to see will reach new heights. Proverbs 25:2 says that,

> *"It is the glory of God to conceal a matter but the glory of kings (or man) is to search out a matter."*

God places great value on our seeking out the things that He conceals. Us this section of the book as a reference tool to spark your mind to think metaphorically. Press in and press on dear saints. The Lord desires to speak to you!

CHAPTER 2

Angels

Remember, angels are here to help and minister to us. They are messengers of God sent to declare God's purpose for your life and destiny. Angels are warriors of God and fight on behalf of the Saints of the Most High. They are actively engaged in the purposes of the Kingdom of God. In book two of this series, "The Seer and Healing," I address the topic of angels at great length.

Angels can come to us in many ways. You may see or discern their presence during worship. You may physically encounter an angel. The writer of Hebrews states,

> *"Do not forget to entertain strangers, for by so doing some have unwittingly entertained angels."*

- Hebrews 13:2

Angels can come to you in a dream or see them in a vision. The following are just a few of the possible reasons for angelic visitation.

Declaration or Proclamation: Angels are messengers sent by God to speak and declare truth regarding some aspect of your life. They come to confirm and proclaim your destiny and call of God. They take God's word over your life and speak it into your spirit. This is a solidifying moment. God wants you to receive and understand his word for you. This is seen throughout the scriptures.

Direction and Guidance: Angels can come with specifics regarding guidance or direction. They may tell you what to do or where to go. They may give you wisdom or insight about something you are going through. In Acts 8:26, an angel spoke to Philip and gave him direction on where to go.

Faith, Healing, and Deliverance: Angels can come to impart to you a level of anointing or to release faith into your life. Faith is the fuel that activates your spirit into action. The Word says that without faith it is impossible to please God. We see Sarai's faith ignited in Genesis 16:7-11.

Angels can come and minister healing (See John 5). Angels can come and bring deliverance. In Psalm 34:7 it says,

> *"The angel of the Lord encamps all around those who fear Him, and delivers them."*

In Isaiah 63:9 we read,

> *"In all their affliction He was afflicted, and the Angel of His Presence saved them; In His love and in His pity He redeemed them; And He bore them and carried them all the days of old."*

Protection or Warning: Angels can be sent to warn you (Matthew 1:20; 2:13; 19-20) or bring protection in a time of need. They are sent to show you how to react or what to do regarding an impending harmful situation. You may see angels engaged in battle on your behalf. When you see this type of activity, pray in prayers of intersession. In Psalm 91:11-12 reads,

> *"For He shall give His angels charge over you, to keep you in all your ways. In their hands they shall bear you up, lest you dash your foot against a stone."*

Revelation and Understanding: Angels can come bringing revelation and prophetic insight. An angel communicated the entire book of Revelation to John. Daniel experienced such incredible Revelation that only an angel could interpret it for him (see Daniel 8:15-26; 9:20-27).

Strength and Comfort: Angels can come to you to impart strength or give you comfort. Angels came to strengthen

Jesus after Hid 40 day fast (See Matthew 4:11; Mark 1:13). Daniel experienced the strength of God through angels (Daniel 10:18). Elijah, after he defeated the prophets of baal (1 Kings 19:5-8).

Worship or ushering in the presence of God: Angels can change the atmosphere of a place and usher in the presence of God. They were created to worship God and they carry with them the atmosphere of Heaven. God's holiness is so vast it electrifies the atmosphere of a place with holiness. Angels cannot help but bring the weightiness of His holiness when they show up.

Animals

Animal symbols are interesting. The animal kingdom is wide and diverse. They may be seen in a vision or a dream. What they are doing or your interaction with them is just as important as their species. Remember, everything is about context. Here are a few examples of animals and their possible meaning.

Bats: Often symbolize demonic activity.

Cats: Cats are self-willed, stealthy or sneaky, and untrainable. Seeing a cat may speak of attitudinal adjustments that need to be made in your life. They are predators and prowl around in search for pray. A black cat may speak of demonic activity.

Deer: Deer are tranquil and can often speak of comfort, peace, or longing (see Psalm 42:1).

Dogs: Dogs can be positive representing fellowship, companionship like that of a brother, or faithfulness. On the other hand they can represent unbelievers or evil men (Psalm 22:16). Dogs that are growling or barking can represent demonic attack or oppression.

Donkey: A donkey can represent the spirit of deception (Numbers 22:22). They may speak of being stubborn or mulish (Job 11:12) or, on the other hand, they may speak of humility (Luke 19:28-44). A donkey can also mean harvest such as plowing or working a farm. A donkey with a pack on its back may mean burdens and worry, the weight of the world on your shoulders.

Fox: Seeing a fox can represent one who is crafty or cunning (Luke 13:332). It can also represent the demonic, robbing the hen house of those newly born again.

Frogs: Frogs often represent the demonic (Revelation 16:13-14). However, they can also represent agility such as a frog leaping across a pond on Lilly pads or compliancy and a sleepish soul such as a frog swimming in a pot of boiling water.

Goats: Goats often represent the demonic, occult, false prophet, or the lost (Matthew 25:33).

Horse: A horse often represents strength, power, or conquest; a horse ready for battle is a good example. Horses can also represent your ministry or God calling you to join His army.

Lamb or Sheep: Sheep and lambs represent Christ or His people (Psalm 78:71; John 10:15). You may see Jesus caring for a sheep, or leaving the 99 to pursue the one. He loves and cares for the sheep of His fold. For example, if you see Jesus shaving a sheep, it may mean He is cleaning you up and striping away the debris in your life.

Lion: A Lion can represent Jesus and His royalty (Psalm 17:12). On the other hand, it may represent the enemy seeking to devour you (1 Peter 5:8).

Ox or Bull: An ox can symbolize service, harvest as in farming, slaughter (Proverbs 7:22), or strength (Proverbs 14:4). Bulls on the other hand can symbolize persecution, spiritual warfare, opposition, or threat (Psalm 22:12).

Aroma

Often, in a vision, dream, or even in the natural you may smell an aroma or a fragrance. Pay attention to the smell. Aromas are vast and their meaning is just as vast. They can usher in the presence of the Lord or tap your history or heritage and bring comfort. They can symbolize warning or atmospheric conditions. The following is just a sample of some of the aromas you may experience:

Cooking odors: Often cooking aromas come from your personal experience and draw upon memories that are meaningful to you. The smell of cinnamon and apples may bring you the comfort of your mother. Smelling the aromas of an outdoor BBQ may signal times of fellowship and family unity. Sweet aromas may be a call to go deeper into your intimacy with the Lord.

Floral aromas: Can symbolize the presence of Christ (Song of Solomon 3:6) or the love of God in your life (Ephesians 5:2). For example, the smell of roses can symbolize God pouring out His love and blessing on a person or an increase of His presence in the atmosphere of a gathering.

Foul odors: Can symbolize demonic activity or sin. For example, smelling rotten eggs (sulfuric) may be a call to intercede and change the atmosphere, binding the demonic from a situation or place.

Seductive aromas: Perfume can symbolize a warning regarding temptation, seduction, or deception (Proverbs 7:7, 10, 13; Ecclesiastes 10:1).

Art

Artistic symbols are fascinating. The range from paintings to sculptures, clay to wood and completed works to works in progress. Art is always about beauty. They can be personal or prophetic. They can symbolize transformation, sanctification, or mission.

The artist is just as important as the art. You may see something that you are painting or you may see Jesus sculpting clay. The first speaks of your dreams and your destiny the latter speaks of Christ's work in your life.

What is being created or painted is also significant. Is it a landscape, a city, or a person? Pay attention to the details. Paintings can also mean "covering." For example, you may see your house being painted speaking to you being covered by His presence or renovating so to speak you as the temple of the Holy Spirit.

A potter's wheel is symbolic of being molded or shaped. Pottery is symbolic of a Godly vessel. Painting can also be negative such as a whitewashed tomb (Matthew 23:27). Context is everything.

Authority Figures

Authority symbols may include your boss, a parent, teacher, guardian, law enforcement, official, judge, politician, or doctor. Each of which carries its own meaning and is often easily understood. Consider the following:

Attorney: Seeing yourself as an attorney can be a call to stand in the gap for a people group and intercede on their behalf. Jesus is not only our Judge (Psalm 51:4) he is our Advocate (1 John 21:1) and in Christ all judgment has passed through Him and. He has freed us from the power of sin and death.

Boss: Seeing your boss may symbolize your relationship with authority. All authority is given and ordained by God (Romans 13:1-3). We are called to be servants to all. Your ability to honor those in authority is critical to being mature and having a heart this is in right relationship with those around us.

Counselor: Seeing a counselor may represent not only the need for getting personal counsel, but may be His desire for you to receive the Holy Spirit, our counselor. In Isaiah 9:6 Jesus is called our Counselor. Jesus referred to the Holy Spirit as the Counselor (John 14:16 AMP).

Doctor: Jesus is our Great Physician (Luke 5:31). Seeing a doctor can range from the need to be healed and God's desire to touch you to being called to the ministry of healing. See medical for more symbols regarding healing.

Judge: The context of seeing a judge can range from standing before the judgment seat of Christ (Romans 14:10) to seeing balances (Psalm 62: 9), a courtroom, or standing before a judge. Often forgiveness is at the heart of the situation. A judge can also symbolize God making a judgment regarding a situation you are going through.

Jury: Seeing a Jury can speak to the weighing of evidence or passing judgment (James 5:9).

Law Enforcement: Seeing officials in this arena represent earthly or spiritual authority (1 Peter 2:13). Depending on the context, it can point to a violation in your life and God is graciously warning you to turn and change your ways. A jailer on the other hand may point to being oppressed by the demonic. Being in Jail can symbolize being in bondage spiritually or mentally.

Teacher: Seeing a teacher often points to being teachable and seeking knowledge and wisdom. Jesus is referred to as our Teacher (Matthew 23:10). Jesus refers to the Holy Spirit as our Teacher (Luke 12:12; John 14:26,

> *"But the Helper, the Holy Spirit, whom the Father will send in My name, He will teach you all things, and brings to remembrance all things that that I said to you.".*

Parent or Guardian: Seeing a parent may represent the need for reconciliation, generational blessing, or inner healing. However, a parent can also represent God.

Sometimes seeing your mother may represent the Holy Spirit and His desire to nurture and comfort you. Likewise, seeing your father may represent Father God and His desire to heal the Father - Child relationship.

Pastor: Seeing your pastor or a pastor can have several meanings. You may be called as a pastor. You may need to deepen you relationship with your pastor. God may be calling you to care for and build your relationship with the flock of God.

CHAPTER 3

B

Birth, Pregnancy, Babies, and Children

Symbolism involving pregnancy, birth, babies, and children are vast and range from having a child in the natural to God birthing something new in your life. Here are a few symbols with their possible meaning.

Adoption: Romans 8:15-17 says,

> *"For you did not receive the spirit of bondage again to fear, but you received the Spirit of adoption by whom we cry out, "Abba, Father." The Spirit Himself bears witness with our spirit that we are children of God, and if children, then heirs—heirs of God and joint heirs with Christ, if indeed we suffer with Him, that we may also be glorified together."*

God has adopted us. We are part of the Royal family of heaven. Adoption speaks to your identity in Christ. He is a father to the fatherless. Our destiny is in Christ as dear sons (Romans 8:15).

Baby or Infant: We know that babies are a gift from God (Psalm 127:3) and that often they symbolize something new God is doing in your life. However, babies are also dependent, helpless, innocent, and sometimes messy. Babies take a lot of work. They need to be fed and nurtured (1 Corinthians 3:1).

Every new work, in its beginning is the same way. It takes time, patience, and perseverance. God may be calling you to use be a wise parent and train care for this new thing like an infant. God may also be calling you to be dependent upon Him like a baby and nourish yourself on the milk of His word.

Child or Children: Children can often symbolize childlike faith and a call to simplicity and faith. God wants us to be as little children, to be filled with innocence, faith, and joy in Him. He wants or trust and dependence to be on Him. He wants to comfort us like a father to a child and release joy and playfulness in your spirit.

Giving Birth and Labor Pain: Giving birth often symbolizes the dream or ministry is about to take place. Often travail, struggle and pain accompany the birthing of a new thing. It calls for perseverance and endurance.

What God has spoken to you in private is now ready to be manifested to the world.

If you see, for example, an umbilical cord can signify the need to detach yourself from something or to cutoff an aspect or occupation in your life. Labor can also symbolize great pain and travail (Jeremiah 6:24).

Miscarriage or Abortion: Symbols regarding a miscarriage or abortion may be speaking to a personal healing that needs to take place in your life. On the other hand, it could represent a graceful warning regarding a work in your life that needs change. Head in one direction and dreams are aborted; head in another direction and the child come to full term.

Pregnancy: Seeing yourself or someone else pregnant may refer to a desire to have a child and God's desire to fulfill that dream. However, more often than not, it refers to God planting the seed of a dream or ministry in your life (Isaiah 42:9; 66:9). Pregnancy is a time of intimacy with the Lord. It is a season to nurture your dream and envision its scope and attributes, what it will look like, who it will touch, how it will function.

Beverages, Drinking

The symbolism of beverages or drinking is vast and can range from drinking living water from the cup of His hand to being bound by addiction. Here are a few common examples.

Alcohol: Drinking alcohol can symbolize a struggle with addiction or residue from a former addiction (Proverbs 20:1). It can also speak of being controlled or under the influence of the demonic, playing the fool, being rebellious, or even witchcraft (Ephesians 5:18; Proverbs 14:16). Being in a bar speaks to a bad or worldly environment.

Simple Beverages: Drinking simple cool beverages can speak of refreshing and good news (proverbs 25:25). For example drinking champagne can symbolize victory, celebration, or christening (to send out).

Vinegar: Drinking vinegar can speak of being mocked or slandered (Psalms 69:21; Matthew 27:48).

Water and Wine: Water and wine, are powerful symbols. The first miracle by Jesus in the book of John was changing water to wine at the wedding in Cana (John 2). Water and wine are powerful images of the church, His bride, being filled with the Spirit of God. Water also speaks of new life in Christ and being filled to overflowing with living water (John 4:7-15; 7:38). Of course, wine speaks of the redemptive work of Christ on the cross and the power of the blood (Matthew 26:28).

When we see the cup of blessing often God is calling us to live in the fullness of the salvation we have received and to be filled with new wine, to be as it were drunk in His Spirit with power and anointing.

Water of Service: We also see water as a symbol of service and the call to serve (John 13:5; Matthew 10:42). This can be a powerful call to missions and to the poor.

Birds

Birds are powerful symbols. Their meaning is wide and vast. Consider the following:

Bird (Singular): I single bird may speak of a messenger or an angel of the Lord. A wounded bird can symbolize the weak under attack or being harmed (Ecclesiastes 10:22).

Birds (Flock): A flock of birds can symbolize the enemy (Matthew 13:4). Or, on the other hand, speak to a people group flocking to the branches of your ministry (Luke 13:19).

Bird Nest: A bird's nest speaks of nurturing the young or one's house and family (Proverbs 27:8).

Bluebirds, Robins: Can symbolize obedience to God and being a faithful servant (Jeremiah 8:7). Bluebirds or Robins can also speak of Holiness and an invitation to come into His presence.

Cardinals: Cardinals can speak of a mainline denomination of the church, such as God doing a work in the Catholic Church.

Crow, Vulture, Buzzard, Raven: This category often speaks of the enemy, for example a crow mocking, a vulture or buzzard circling the dead or dying, or a raven standing in the road as you travel.

Dove: Doves usually speak of the Holy Spirit descending to anoint, to be filled (Luke 3:22), or to be called.

Eagle, Hawk, Owl: In general, birds of prey speak of the prophetic, seeing from the heavens (Isaiah 9:11). Of course an Eagle symbolizes Christ (Ezekiel 1:10; Revelation 4:7). Owls speak of the prophetic. Owls symbolize how an individual is gifted to peer into the dark places.

Hen: A hen can symbolize God's desire to comfort His children (Luke 13:34).

Hummingbirds: Can symbolize evangelism, pollinating flowers with great speed and urgency.

Parrot: On the positive side, a parrot can symbolize beauty. On the negative side, a parrot can symbolize someone who mimics the works and deeds of another.

Pigeon: A pigeon can symbolize folks being feed from the hand of your ministry as in feeding pigeons in a park. A pigeon can also symbolize a messenger or angel delivering a message, as in a homing pigeon.

Roadrunner: A roadrunner can symbolize a warrior, one who fights in the dry places and devours the enemy (snakes). The can also speak to moving fast and staying alert.

Songbird: Songbirds can speak of love or adoration, and is often a call to dive deeper into worship.

Sparrow: Sparrows can symbolize the poor and needy and a call to feed and care for them (Psalm 84:3). It can also speak to loneliness, solitude, or quietness (Psalm 102:7). It can also speak of God's provision (Matthew 10:29).

Stork: A stork can symbolize the birth of something new in your life or finding your home or locking into your destiny (Jeremiah 8:7). It can also speak of angels (Zechariah 5:9).

Swallow: A swallow speaks of peace, rest, and worship, or resting in the house of God (Psalm 84:3). A Swallow can also speak to a need to return to fellowship and the house of worship.

Blood

Blood is a powerful symbol. It points to Christ and the power of the blood of Jesus (Matthew 26:28). Losing blood can speak to the need to put your trust and faith in Christ (Luke 8:43). Walking in blood can symbolize the power of Christ saturating every step that you take. A blood transfusion speaks of regeneration, salivation, and deliverance (Titus 3:5; Romans 12:2).

Body Parts

Symbols that focus on a part of the body are powerful. If it is a vision, it may be a word of knowledge for healing or a spiritual condition of a person. On the other hand, they could symbolize faith, weakness, power, strength, or wisdom. Consider the following:

Ankles: Can symbolize weak faith (Ezekiel 47:3) or the need to stabilize your walk with God.

Arms: Can symbolize God's strength (Psalm 89:13; Isaiah 62:8.) Arms can also symbolize giving aid or reaching out, and deliverance (Isaiah 52:10; Psalm 136:12). They can also speak to God having the power to save and meet you need (Numbers 11:23).

Back: Seeing a back can symbolize God desiring you to seek His face (Exodus 34, 34). It may also speak to having feelings of being ignored or someone turning their back against you (Jeremiah 32:33). Seeing a back can also symbolize the need for healing as in by His stripes we were healed (1 Peter 2:24, Isaiah 53:5).

Body: Can symbolize your relationship to fellow members of the church or the equipping of the saints (Romans 12:4; 1 Corinthians 12:12; Ephesians 4:4). It can also symbolize you being the temple of the Holy Spirit and a call to Glorify God in your body and your spirit (1 Corinthians 6:19).

Bones: Can symbolize the lost, being backslidden, or a dead church or member (Matthew 23:27; Ezekiel 37). Bones can also speak to weakness, fear, or a need for God to heal you (Isaiah 58:11; Proverbs 16:24; Proverbs 3:8). It can also symbolize a broken spirit (Proverbs 17:22). Alternatively, it may speak to bringing good news (Proverbs 15:30; 16:24). Bones can also speak of revival and the need to intercede on the behalf of a people group.

Ear: Ears speak to hearing God (Matthew 11:15). They can also speak to His desire to give you a hearing ear as in the prophetic. Being deaf can speak to opening your heart and hearing what the Lord has to say (Acts 28:27).

Feet, Foot: Feet often speak of service and personal ministry (John 13:1, Romans 10:15). Feet can also represent God telling you to "shake of" hurt or rejection (Matthew 10:14). Laying something down at Jesus's feet can speak of worship (Luke 7:38) and giving up your own personal desires (Matthew 18:29; 28:9, Mark 7:25). Feet can also symbolize the Lord guiding you in your walk (Luke 1:79; Psalm 40:2; 56:14). Feet can symbolize God's protection (1 Samuel 2:9; Psalm 18:33, 36, 38). Feet can speak of the authority you have in

Christ (Psalm 8:6). Stand on the power of His Word (Psalm 119:101).

Looking at your feet can speak to examining your walk with God (Proverbs 4:26). I often see the feet of Jesus and the call to walk where He walks, to do what He is doing and to see what He is seeing. Footprints can speak to Christ walking with you even if you do not see Him or recognize He is there (i.e. footprints in the sand).

Finger: A finger can mean casting out a demon or the power of God (Luke 11:20). A pointing finger can speak of being an accuser or speaking wicked or harmful things (Isaiah 58:9).

Hair: Grey hair or a beard symbolizes old age or wisdom (Proverbs 16:31). Long hair can symbolize a call to the prophetic, like a Nazarite (Numbers 6:2; Judges 13:5). Baldness can symbolize not being covered or not having protection from God (Micah 1:16).

Hand: Hands are powerful. If your hands are lifted, it speaks of surrender and worship (Psalm 28:2; 63:4). If your hands are folded, it speaks of prayer. Holding hands speak of love and relationship (Psalm 37:24). Washing your hands speaks of being cleansed from sin (Psalm 24:4, 6). Strong hands speak of being made ready to war in the Spirit (Psalm 18:34).

Clapping hands speak of praise (Psalm 47:1). Hands can also speak of angelic protection (Psalm 91:12). A left hand can symbolize wisdom (Proverbs 3:16). An open hand can speak of God's grace (Psalm 123:2). An extended right hand can speak of agreement or a partnership. Trembling hands can speak of fear. Hands that cover your face can speak of shame.

Hands often speak to me about being an extension of Christ's mighty hand in the earth. His hands become my hands. The works of His hands are mighty and call for our adoration, worship, and praise.

Head: A head bowed can speak to humility, shame, or prayer and that God is the lifter of your head (Psalm 3:3; Job 10:15; Zachariah 6:11). A head receiving a crown speaks of your place in the kingdom of God, your royal nature in Him, and the wisdom of God (Psalm 22:7; Proverbs 4:9). A hand under your head speaks of Christ embrace and love for you (Song of Songs 2:6).

The head also speaks of authority. Christ is the head of all things (Ephesians 1:22); He is the head of the Church (Colossians 1:18), and head over all principality and power (Ephesians 2:10). The Husband is the head of the family (Ephesians 5:23). A wounded head is the call to be healed emotionally.

A covered head speaks to covering and relationship to authority. Wrinkles on the forehead can speak to worry or thoughts. A lifted head can speak to seeking the Lord in prayer and supplication or His glory and seeking His face.

Heart: A heart can speak of many things but usually speaks to a heart condition such as a broken heart (Psalm 34:18), joyous heart (Psalm 16:19, Acts 2:26), fools heart (Psalm 14:1), pure heart (Psalm 24:4), wicked heart (Psalm 10:13, Acts 5:3, Acts 7:51), clean heart (Psalm 51:10), sorrowful heart (John 16:6), or a critical heart (Psalm 12:2). Everything starts with the heart (Matthew 5; 12:34, Romans 2:29). Salvation and faith start with the heart (Romans 10:9-10). Doing God's will starts with the heart (Ephesians 6:6).

Your heart is the place of overflowing (John 7:38). Heartstrings can speak of pulling on the heartstrings of Christ. A bleeding heart can mean either be compassion or being mocked because of your service to Christ. You may see a heart darkened (hurt or deceived), a heart beating (the passion of Christ), and blood flowing through a heart (moving out in the power of Christ).

Legs: Legs can speak of strength or weakness (Daniel 2:33) as well as your walk or journey in Christ as in seeing legs walking.

Books, Scrolls, Letters, Writing

Seeing books, scrolls, letters, or writing can be very powerful to your life. As you will see below, their meaning is wide yet pointed.

Books: Books are powerful and their meaning can often be derived by the title, if visible. Often, a book speak of the Word of God, and its power to build you up and guide you in all truth. The Word of God is the revelation of Jesus Christ. The Word speaks to truth (John 17:11, Psalm 33:4). Jesus Himself is the Word incarnate (John 1:1). Seeing the Bible and the wind blowing upon the pages speak to the power of God's word and the authority of Him to bring about what He has spoken.

Often you will see a scripture highlighted. Take note and meditate upon it. Seeing the book of life can speak to the need for salvation (Revelation 20:12). Seeing books can also be a call to study the scriptures (Daniel 9:2). Sometime books can be a graceful admonishment to balance your life between study and living the gospel (Ecclesiastes 12:12). Burning books can symbolize the renunciation of occult practices or witchcraft (Acts 19:19).

Letters: Letters are interesting and involve reading, writing, sending, or receiving a letter. Often what is being written can tell you the meaning of the letter. If you are writing a letter, ask yourself what is the tone of the letter;

Do you have a need to communicate to someone in some way? Letters can be many things, love letters, letters of endorsement, encouragement, admonishment, or a teaching. They can bring good news or speak prophetically. Receiving a letter can be an answer to a prayer or a call to go to a people group or nation. Seeing letters as in the alphabet can speak to words of proclamation or a word of knowledge.

Scrolls: A scroll can carry the same meaning as the Bible (Psalm 40:7). A scroll can also speak of judgment (Isaiah 30:8), proclaiming the prophetic (Isaiah 8:1; Jeremiah 36:1, Ezekiel 2:9, 3:2), or a call to preach and proclaim the Word. A flying scroll can be either a curse (Zechariah 5) or the Word being sent to a nation.

Seeing Jesus reading a scroll in a courtroom or before the throne of God can symbolize His decree over your life and the proclamation of forgiveness. An open scroll extending from heaven to earth can symbolize God's decree being manifest or His Word ushering you into heaven and His presence.

Being Bound

Being bound by handcuffs or any other type of binding speaks of being in bondage, to stop certain behaviors, or to release someone from bondage. Binding loosing speaks to doing the works of the Kingdom (Matthew 16:19).

Bugs, Insects

Insects are interesting and typically speak of demonic activity (flies, locusts, cockroaches, spiders, bug bites, maggots, swarming insects, etc.). These types of insects devour, trap, poison, impart diseases, or inhabit a dirty environment.

However, bugs can also speak of good things. For example, ants can speak of being industrious, bees can speak of evangelism and pollination, and caterpillars can speak of transformation as into a butterfly, butterflies can speak of a season of transformation and beauty. Grasshoppers can speak of God's promise to restore loss in your life (Joel 2:25) or speak to an impending attack on the harvest of your ministry.

Buildings & Houses

Buildings and houses can speak of many things, for example an abandoned house can speak to barrenness and desolation (Job 15:28). A house can also speak to the state of your life and/or past. A barn can refer to abundance, provision, or great harvest (Proverbs 3:9; Psalm 144:13; Jeremiah 50:26; Luke 12:24). A log cabin or camping in a tent could symbolize the need to find a quiet time or be in a secluded place. A tent or a hotel can also symbolize being in a temporary place (Exodus 14:1).

A castle can symbolize a stronghold in someone's life. A cave can symbolize being trapped (Isaiah 42:2), doing something in secret, or hiding in fear like Elijah.

A house with an exposed foundation, or a house sitting on a rock or in sand refers to the condition of trust in a person's life (Matthew 7:24-27).

A house of cards speaks to folly. A cluttered house speaks of the need to put your house in order. Building a house can symbolize the building of a church or ministry. A house with holes in the roof can speak of areas in your life that are in need of repair.

A shack can speak of self-worth or a need for inner healing or trust. Sometimes seeing building can symbolize the need for shelter, refuge or safety.

A tower can be a refuge (Psalm 61:3) or an attic speaks to your mind. A bedroom speaks of intimacy. A closet can speak of prayer (Luke 8:17) or a place where you bury things or hide things.

Chapter 4

C

Celebration

Celebration can be seen in symbols such as people clapping, watching a parade, a ribbon cutting ceremony, a birthday cake, toasting with a glass of wine, people raising to their feet, or seeing colorful balloons or presents.

Cleaning & Cleaning Agents

Seeing anything related to cleaning such as cleaning agents or cleaning equipment (brooms) can speak to cleaning your life up (Isaiah 14:23; Psalm 26:6; John 13:8).

Colors

Many times colors have significance in dreams or visions. I have seen paint being poured over individuals, or candles with different colored flames signifying a gift or a call on the life of a believer. Below is a brief list of some possible meanings:

Blue, Purple, and Scarlet: These three represent the colors of the Godhead. In Exodus blue, purple and scarlet are mentioned 25 times, all referencing the thread used in weaving the elements of the tabernacle. Blue is symbolic of the Holy Spirit and speaks of the wind of God. Purple speaks to the Father and His royal nature. Scarlet speaks of the Son and the blood of Christ.

Blue: Speaks to holiness, heaven, grace, favor, heavenly activity, anointing. Blue can also speak of being depressed or feeling blue. Blue is often a call to holiness and revelation in the prophetic.

Black: Speaks to the enemy, the atmosphere influenced by the enemy, a dark heart, black eyes, dark shadows, speak to evil influence in a person or place.

Brown: Speaks to things in the natural, earthly things or a condition or change in a region, or natural qualities. Brown often a call to uncharted areas – a mission gift.

Green: Green speaks to life, growth, prosperity, or renewal, for example, a brown and dusty land being transformed into green grassy lands. Green is often a call to evangelism.

Gray: Speaks of wisdom or can speak to a gray area or an infusion of the enemy in a situation. Gray can also speak of an emotional state such fogginess. Gray is often a call to teach as in gray hair.

Orange: Speaks to either caution as in an orange light or the fire of anointing and power in the Spirit. It is often a call to healing.

Purple: Speaks of heavenly royalty and your kingdom identity.

Red: Symbolizes sacrifice, danger, the blood of Christ to over through the enemy, or even anger. Red is often a call to intersession and pleading the blood of Christ over the nations or a call to Apostleship.

Scarlet: Refers to the blood of Christ or possible a sin in someone's life.

White: Speaks of righteousness and holiness before God. Can often speak to a high call of worship.

Yellow: Speaks to the gift of God, something precious and with great value. It carries with it the idea of family, honor, and celebration. On the negative side, it can refer to cowardliness or fear and intimidation. Yellow is often a call to service and releasing anointing.

Communication

In today's world methods of communication is everywhere. You might see a phone, cell phone, answering machine, e-mail, antenna, radio, newspaper, or mailbox. At the heart of this type of symbolism is the call to listen. They often carry the idea of hearing what God is saying - to tune into to Him.

On the other extreme, you may see things like a microphone, a platform, or a speaker. This speaks to proclamation and speaking to a people group or a person regarding the Gospel or the prophetic.

Confinement

Confinement can be in a jail, cage, dungeon, pit, or some other place where you or someone else is trapped. This speaks to being either stuck or being in bondage or under oppression, taken prisoner by the enemy (Jeremiah 5:26-27; Isaiah 42:7).

Being bound by chains, locks, or a straightjacket carry the same type of meaning. The latter may speak to mental bondage. Jesus came to set the captives free.

Construction, Building Something

Seeing something being built or constructed often speaks to building God's call in your life, working to fulfill your destiny. Often this involves tearing down (Jeremiah 4:3; Hosea 10:12), establishing a solid foundation, setting up the framework, putting in the infrastructure, and counting the cost (1 Corinthians 3:10-12; Luke 14:28).

On the other hand, if you see bricks this can symbolize bondage or slavery (Exodus 5). A carpenter can speak to the office of a pastor, evangelist, or apostle.

Containers (all kinds)

Containers are vast; there are containers that carry things, containers to drink from, containers that hold things, and containers that lock things away. Below is a list of a few examples of containers and their possible meaning:

Containers that carry:

- A basket full of fruit can speak to provision, harvest or blessing being brought to a people group.

- A basket filled with bread can speak to bringing the Word to a people group or feeding the poor and needy.
- A vessel filled with wine speaks to God's desire to pour out His Spirit upon a group and fill them with new wine.
- A briefcase can speak to a call to the business community.
- A suitcase can speak of a journey and being sent out.
- Luggage can speak to carrying around the residue of your past and speak to the need for inner healing.
- A bucket overflowing may speak to renewal and outpouring.

Containers for drinking: Seeing cups, glasses, or bottles filled with water or wine speaks to being filled with the Holy Spirit and the possible need to be refreshed in Him. God's desire is that your cup would overflow and bless many. A broken vessel or a vessel that is leaking, such as a cracked pot can symbolize a crack in your foundation, or running on empty and the need to be filled with His Spirit and repair an aspect of your life. Wineskins speak of your spiritual structure (Luke 5:37).

Containers that hold something: Seeing a treasure chest, a safe, or safe-deposit box speaks of provision, blessing, and favor, but can also mean something that is hidden. Containers that hold something can also speak to storing away for times of famine.

Containers that bind and hold: Containers that secure things away such as a spider in a jar, a snake in a basket, or like Zechariah's basket with a woman in it, spoke of God judging the harlotry of the nation (Zechariah 5) or binding the enemy.

Dirty vessels: Speaks to the need to be cleansed so that you can be filled to the fullness of Christ and not be hindered in your walk. Glass, in general speaks to transparency.

Cooking

Cooking is amazing in its symbolism. As a chef by trade, the Lord often draws from the well of my life experiences and uses cooking and food to speak to my heart. To get a glimpse of this I encourage you to read my book, "The Eyes of a Chef, Kitchen Tales of Food & Faith" (available on Amazon.com). In addition, throughout this series I share quite a few stories that are drawn from the well of my life experience walking with God.

Cooking is so vast and ranges from savory to sweet, baking to roasting, cold food preparation including working with forcemeats (sausages, pates) to carving ice or making chocolate sculptures. Cooking is about preparation. It starts with raw ingredients and transforms them into something that can be consumed. Thus, the symbolism often speaks to what God is doing in your life or the life of another.

Butchering, filleting, cutting, and carving often speak to things being cut away, works of the flesh, or areas of your life that need to be removed.

Recipes can speak to great truths in scripture. for example, a simple preparation of hollandaise sauce points to the sacrifice of Jesus and His redemptive work on the cross; making a consommé speaks to the sanctifying work of the Holy Spirit; or making bread speaks to God building the framework in your life to sustain a filling of the Holy Spirit.

The metaphors are endless. I encourage you to let the Holy Spirit speak to you regarding your own profession, or ask Him to open your eyes when you prepare food for your family and friends, and share with them what He shows you at the table of fellowship.

Simmering, slow roasting, kneading dough, or stewing often speak to that slow sanctifying work of the Holy Spirit in your life.

Tasting, smelling, aroma, fragrance, and seasoning, can speak to the power of His Word in your life to the beauty of His presence.

Covering and Mantles

Mantels speak to the "metron" (sphere of influence and the boundaries of one's authority, Ephesians 4:7) of your anointing, ministry, or office.

Coverings speak to your place under authority and under God. The symbols that speak to coverings include things like feathers, blankets, hats, a roof, sheets, a tent, or umbrella.

Symbols that speak to mantels include things like a robe, cape, jacket, coat, or scarf. When they are combined with a color, they can give insight into the meaning. Pay attention of its condition (clean or dirty, whole or torn).

Crime

Seeing crime being committed when it's happening to you or someone else often speaks of an attack by the enemy. The type of crime can indicate what is being done. For example, being robbed or stealing speaks to the enemy taking away something that God has given you. it can be as simple as stealing your peace to trying to rob you of your destiny. Cheating, rape, or other crimes can symbolize a violation in a relationship. Gangs can symbolize the atmosphere of a region and a stronghold of the enemy. Murder can speak to the enemy coming in to rob life and bring despair and hopelessness.

Crushed, Carried, Trapped, Stuck, Smothered

Symbols regarding things that are happening to you, or to someone else, are often about God's desire to release you from a circumstance or an emotional condition. For example, you may see yourself being crushed by a rock or trapped under a log. Situations like this speak to emotional stress over a situation where you feel there is no way out and your hope is dissipating. God desires to release you and set you free. Pay attention to your feelings in a dream. Feelings often accompany images and are part of the context. Visions regarding this type of activity are usually words of knowledge.

Being crushed or smothered: At the heart of this symbol is the sense of being overwhelmed by a situation or crushed by the power of a sin in your life. Powerlessness and panic set in and you feel there is no way out. God's desire is to release you and free you from the situation. Freedom is His heartbeat for you. Emotional distress in your life points to being out of balance and susceptible to the power of fear. No this, perfect love casts out fear!

Being stuck or trapped: The meaning is pretty much the same as above, except for one possible exception. It may speak to your reaction to a season of stagnancy in your life. In seasons like this God is calling you to a deeper place of trust. He wants the peace of His presence to sustain you. He wants your hope to rest in Him. He is faithful and dry seasons are times to build your trust and ability to stand in any situation.

Being carried: Being carried often symbolizes God's protection, comfort, and ability to carry you through a situation. Think about that simple and profound story of "foot prints in the sand." He is the Good Shepard and He cares for the flock of His inheritance.

CHAPTER 5

D

Digging

Digging often symbolizes searching out something or digging for a deeper relationship with God. You may be digging for water (His presence or search the Word), for oil (His anointing), or for gold (His provision). The essence of digging is the same as "hunger" or "thirst". It is the cry of ones heart to go deeper in Him.

However, sometimes it is not digging in the sense to find, but to release. I once saw one of our founding fathers digging. I asked the Lord what he was digging for and He said, "*He is not digging, he is releasing the gift of heritage and inheritance upon the land.*" In that case, it spoke to inheritance and the releasing of blessing to the nation.

Direction

Seeking direction from the Lord is common to all who love Him and desire to be where He is. The Lord speaks many different ways regarding direction. Sometimes they involve instruments like a compass, weathervane, road sign, or a map. Other times He uses the road itself, such as a forked road, rocky road, hilly road, a path in a valley, a mountain road, or a freeway.

The context of what you see and the other things going on around you will dictate its meaning. You are looking for things that signify if you are headed in the right direction, wrong direction, or a new uncharted course. Dead ends speak to heading in the wrong direction. Things like road signs, a wall at the end of a road, a closed road, or even the corner of a house or room can symbolize the wrong direction or dead end.

Doors, Gates, Windows

This category of symbols is very powerful and often carries with it the invitation to enter the heavenlies and into the presence of the Lord. One of the most noted open doors in scripture is found in the book of Revelation:

> *"After these things I looked, and behold, a door standing open in heaven. And the first voice which I heard was like a trumpet speaking with me, saying, "Come up here, and I will show you things which must take place after this. Immediately I was in the Spirit; and behold, a throne set in heaven, and One sat on the throne."*
>
> - Revelation 4:1-2

Obviously, doors, gates, and windows are either open or closed. Doors typically speak to an entrance into something. In the case above, God was inviting John to enter heaven and see what He was seeing. Just three verses earlier, Jesus, speaking to the Laodicean church says, *"Behold, I stand at the door and knock. If anyone hears My voice and opens the door, I will come in to him and dine with him, and he with Me."* In the latter case, the invitation is to open the door of your heart and let Jesus in. Jesus, in fact, refers to Himself as "the door" (John 10:7-9). One is open the other is closed.

Open doors also speak to the Holy Spirit opening a door to a new area, region, or place of effectiveness (1 Corinthians 16:9; 2 Corinthians 2:12; Colossians 4:3; Revelation 3:8). If an animal or person is blocking a door, it speaks to the enemy blocking access and God is calling for intersession.

Gates carry the same thrust of meaning, as seen in Luke 13:24, "*Strive to enter through the narrow gate....*" In Revelation 21:21 we see the New Jerusalem coming down from heaven having twelve gates of pearl. Gates also carry the symbolism of entering the heavenlies with praise and thanksgiving (Psalm 24:7-9, 100:4). We often sing that incredible Jesus Culture song, "*Let it rain... Open the floodgates of heaven and let it rain.*" Here, floodgates speak to revival and renewal.

Gates like doors can also speak to the gates of your heart (Psalm 147:13). The difference between gates and doors is that doors, most often, speak to the things Christ is doing or wants to do in your life, gate most often speak of Him wanting to be with you and involves praise and worship. The exceptions in regards to gates are what I call natural gates such as rod iron, gates in a yard, and gates in a jail. These often speak to bondage or oppression of some kind and the call of God to set someone free.

Windows speak to the blessing and anointing of God being poured out from heaven (Malachi 3:10). That wonderful song, "*Open the Windows of Heaven*", was first pinned in 1895 by R. G. Staples. It was so powerful it moved the church for over a century. Since that time, many songs have been written that beat to the heart cry of God. That cry is not only for blessing, but also for renewal, where our hearts cry out for the rain of heaven to pour down upon us.

Windows can also speak to the windows of your heart and the Lord peering into the deep places of your soul. Windows can also speak to the eyes of your spirit, or insight (Ecclesiastes 12:3), as in the old English proverb speaking of the eyes being the windows to the soul. The state of a window is also important. Is the window dirty or clean, fogged over or clear, whole or cracked? If, for example, you see yourself driving and the windows are dirty, cracked, or are being pounded by rain, and your vision is impaired, this speaks to something in your life that is hindering you from seeing clearly. The same would apply to seeing the windows of your house. On the other hand, if you see, for example stained glass windows, it speaks to the beauty and glory of God in your life.

Paul, speaking on the revelatory gifts says,

> *"For now we see in a mirror, dimly, but then face to face. Now I know in part, but then I shall know just as I also am known."*
>
> - 1 Corinthians 13:12

This mirror or glass carries the same essence as a window, peering into the revelatory, but seeing dimly, or in part. We also see the same type of thing in 2 Corinthians 3:18:

> *"But we all, with unveiled face, beholding as in a mirror [glass] the glory of the Lord, are being transformed into the same image from*

glory to glory, just as by the Spirit of the Lord."

Chapter 6

E-F

Education

Symbolism involving things related to education, learning, or graduating are very powerful and can speak to:

A call (teacher, preacher), Exodus 18:20.

Being called to a campus ministry and to students.

Being tutored in the school of the Holy Spirit (elementary school, or college), Galatians 4:1-3.

Going to the next level (diploma).

Learning something (including apprenticeship, college, library, being a student, etc.).

Passing or taking a test (quiz, test, report card, or grade), James 1:3.

Emotions, Feelings, Reactions

See yourself or someone else getting emotional, displaying feelings, or reacting in an unusual manner often points to possible pain or hurt in one's life. The root of the problem can stem from natural circumstances, past hurts, oppression, or the demonic. They include things like blushing, anger, crying, despair, yelling, hopelessness, or even terror. Pictures such as these can often be a word of knowledge regarding one's emotional state. The Holy Spirit will give insight.

On the other hand, you may see emotions of joy and jubilation. Happiness, peace, and laughing often symbolize the Lord's blessing and favor over a life.

Farming, Planting, Plowing, Harvest

Seeing things relating to farming, plowing, planting and harvest most often speak to what Christ is doing in the earth, releasing waves of grace, salvation, revival, and promise.

Plowing almost always speaks of breaking new ground or turning the soil of your heart. Sometimes God is doing a major work in your life and He may use this symbolism to show the depth of the process. Reaping the harvest speaks to bringing in the lost, however, sometimes it can speak to God's provision.

Grinding wheat speaks to the separation of chaff, and the sanctifying work of the Holy Spirit. On the other hand, seeing farmland that is under a drought or the land is dry, speaks to the spiritual condition of a region or a heart, and is a call to pray for revival rain to soak the land. Notice that the soil can be either a region or the soil of one's heart.

Finance and Provision

Symbols involving finance can speak to a need, provision, warning to save, tithing, or restoration of what was lost. Sometimes the meaning is almost tongue-and-cheek, such as "you can bank on it." Sometimes it speaks to where your real treasure lies (Matthew 6:21, 19:21), or the great heavenly inheritance that is in your life.

At other times, it can speak to safety and security. A calculator can speak to counting the cost of something either spiritually or in the natural (Luke 14:28). A check can speak not only of provision, but also of faithfulness and a return on your work for the Lord (Mark 4:8), or the wages of one's life (Romans 6:23). Coins can symbolize service (Matthew 25:14). Things like a creditor or beggar can symbolize a curse on someone's life (Psalm 109:11).

Fire

Symbols involving fire speak to many things and can be either positive or negative. Here are a few examples:

A fire alarm is a warning of impending trouble in one's life.

A house or basement on fire can speak to one heading to the gates of hell.

Ashes speak to memories or residue in a life and the call to heal the brokenness of the past.

Being a firefighter, holding a fire extinguisher, or putting out a fire is symbolic of warfare and extinguishing the flames of the enemy.

Breathing fire speaks to words spoken harshly or in anger. They are often hurtful and destructive.

Burning coals symbolize cleansing. Walking across burning coals speaks to trial and testing.

Candles speak to light and the work of the Holy Spirit. Sometimes the color of a candle can speak to gifting's and call. A candlestick can also speak to the church.

Feet set ablaze speak of evangelism and taking the Word of God to the streets.

Fire in the eyes can speak to lust of the flesh and evil desire.

Fire falling speak of the fire of God falling – revival fire.

Fire in general can speak to the presence of God or His Word, but can also speak to the road to hell depending on the context.

Hands on fire speak to healing anointing and a call to heal.

Hearts on fire speaks to hunger for God, hearts set ablaze for Him.

Smoke can speak to hindrance that will soon dissipate. Smoke can also speak to a smoke screen from the enemy.

Fish and Fishing

Fish and fishing usually speaks to saving souls and the harvest. There are a few exceptions, for example a fishhook can speak to an area of one's life where the enemy has snagged them and a possible stronghold has rooted itself. Bait can speak to a trap set by the enemy.

Flying

Seeing yourself flying is often symbolic of soaring into His presence and dreaming your destiny. Flight speaks to freedom in the His Spirit and carries with it a call of passionate union with Him.

> *"So I said, "Oh, that I had wings like a dove! I would fly away and be at rest,*
>
> *- Psalms 55:6*

Wings have the same connotation, but can also mean a way out of a situation is being given. It is a call to trust and seek His guidance.

> *"Keep me as the apple of Your eye; Hide me under the shadow of Your wings,"*
>
> *- Psalms 17:8*

Seeing dark shadowy creatures flying speak to the enemy hovering over a situation, person, or place. This is a call to warfare and intersession.

> *'Woe to the land shadowed with buzzing wings,"*
>
> *- Isaiah 18:1*

Food

Food, as a metaphor, is used throughout the Scriptures. Food in general can speak to many things in the Spirit. For example:

Bread often speaks to the bread of His presence or His body being broken for our salvation.

Bread and butter can also speak of God's provision.

Cheese can speak to a season of development in your life where the Lord is taking the curds and salting, pressing, and aging them for His purpose.

Cinnamon is symbolic of anointing and being set apart (Exodus 30:23-25).

Corn often can speak to the prophetic or having ears to hear.

Cream can speak to the richness of what God is doing in you or a group of people (cream in a sea of milk). **Cream being whipped** can speak to being filled or aerated with the Holy Spirit. **Cream being churned** into butter speaks to being anointed for service, to be spread or smeared upon the hot toast of His body, the church.

Cream of Wheat speaks to a rich and abundant harvest.

Eggs can speak to new things being birthed.

Fruit often speaks to the spiritual fruit in your life (Matthew 3:10, 7:17-19. 12:33).

Grapes speak to the community of believers, the church.

Honey or a honeycomb, often speaks to the sweetness of His words and to proclamation, the comb symbolizing a release of the prophetic, or portals of revelation being poured out upon the church.

Meat speaks to the meat of His Word (1 Corinthians 3:2).

Milk often speaks to the milk of the Word of God (1 Corinthians 3:2, Hebrews 5:12-13, 1 Peter 2:2).

Mustard speaks of faith and the power of small beginnings (Matthew 13:31-31).

Salt speaks to the Life of Christ in you and your character (Matthew 5:13).

Sugar and sweets can point to the sweetness of the Holy Spirit or telling people what they want to hear as opposed to telling the truth in love (2 Timothy 4:3).

Chapter 7

G

Garments and Clothing

Clothing and being dressed has powerful symbolism. Pay attention to the type of clothing or what may be out of place, for example:

A run in your stalking or tear in your dress could speak of being violated by a person or, sin, or the demonic.

Jeans with holes in them could speak to poverty and the need for provision.

Pants with no belt could mean the need forth truth in your walk.

Shoes that are too big could speak to how you see yourself in relationship to your call.

The importance of clothing type:

The type of clothing is just as important as what maybe missing. What is the state of the clothing? Are they clean or dirty, new or worn? Color is important. White cloths symbolize righteousness and salvation; dark cloths can mean demonic, bright cloths can speak to your personality, spotted can mean the need to clean up some aspic of your life. Accessories may be important as well. For example:

Apron speaks of service.

Armband speaks of allegiance.

Backpack, baggage, or luggage can symbolize carrying around to many things or worry. Luggage can also symbolize God preparing you to move or take a journey. Or, it may be a burden you carry from the past.

Being naked can symbolize having your life exposed, or feeling embarrassment, or loss.

Boots are often a symbol of war. Being in camouflage can symbolize being stealth in your service.

Coats and jackets can symbolize helping the needy or being comforted, covered, protected, or even a mantel of ministry.

Coattails can speak of being overly attached to a person.

Cowboy attire can mean you do not work well in a team - you are a cowboy and just rush in.

Diapers can speak to sin and the need to be changed.

Dressed in the opposite gender attire may speak to a sin in your life, gender confusion, or being attacked by the enemy.

Earmuffs can mean you do not want to hear something.

Leisure attire can speak to the need for rest.

Mask, costume, or veil can symbolize putting on a front, not being real, deception, or hiding something.

Military uniform or armor speaks of your call as a soldier of Christ and being equipped to do battle (Ephesians 6).

Pair of overalls can speak to you as an evangelist.

Robes speak of royalty and ministry mantels. The color can be significant, gold, blue, purple, or scarlet is symbolic of holiness, glory, and beauty (Exodus. 28:2).

Vests can symbolize the need for protection and God's desire for you to walk in righteousness.

Wedding dress can speak to you as the bride of Christ.

Work cloths can speak to a call in your life to a people group for example a suit may be a call to the world of business.

Gems, Jewels, Jewelry

Gems, jewels, and jewelry speak great worth and value of a person to our King. They carry with it the idea of our royal inheritance in heaven. We are priests and kings in the eyes of Christ. We are pearls of great price, diamonds honed from the rock of humanity and stand at the gate of the Kingdom. Jewels speak to our true riches in heaven (1 Corinthians 3:12).

Rings speak to revival and refreshing and point to use as the Bride of Christ. Being given a ring speaks to a revelation of your identity in Christ. A specific ring with a specific gem can speak to a specific call on someone's life.

Geographic, Nations, and Cities

Seeing cities, nations, or geographic locations speak to many things including intersession for a place or people group, a call to missions or evangelism, discernment regarding atmospheric conditions of a region, life in the Spirit, or a personal state of being. Examples include the following.

Cities under siege: If you see a location and it is dark, shadowy, in ruins, or under attack, this often speaks to the spiritual condition and a call to intercede on behalf of the people living there. This is a warfare stance in prayer (Psalm 74:20).

City set on a hill: This is symbolic of being in Christ and the safety and security of His presence. Think of Cities of Refuge.

Golden City: Seeing symbols that point to the Kingdom of Heaven are often revelatory or a call to enter into His presence (Revelation 21:2).

Hustle and bustle of a city: This can speak to being overworks and overwhelmed, and God is calling you to a place of balance and rest.

Maps, Cities, Nations, and Flags: See a physical location and possibly its condition, most often speaks to pray for that part of the world and may include a call to mission life at that local.

Glory of God

Seeing the Glory of God in a dream or vision is an awe-inspiring event. When an event such as that takes place typically, there are one of two reasons, either God is embracing you at a deep level to draw you in closer and imparting to you something that will greatly impact your commission in life, or you do not know Him and He is graciously wooing you to Himself. In my case, I have experienced both. In book three, of this series you can read about my pre-salvation encounter with the Lord Jesus Christ.

Often in visions or a trance one can be caught up to the throne of God and experience the beauty and glory of the kingdom of God. Paul, in 2 Corinthians 12:1-4, describes his own experience of being caught up to the third heaven:

> *"It is doubtless not profitable for me to boast. I will come to visions and revelations of the Lord: I know a man in Christ who fourteen years ago—whether in the body I do not know, or whether out of the body I do not know, God knows—such a one was caught up to the third heaven. And I know such a man—whether in the body or out of the body I do not know, God knows— how he was caught up into Paradise and heard inexpressible words, which it is not lawful for a man to utter."*

From a Seer's gift standpoint, often during ministry one may see the glory of God resting upon people. This activity can either be a word of knowledge calling for an action, or a discerning of the atmosphere that ushers in God's grace for healings, miracles, signs, and wonders.

We are living in a season where God is breaking through in incredible ways. It is not uncommon for individuals not only to experience the glory of God through visions, trances, dreams, and angelic visitations, but through physical signs that make you wonder, all of which are stirring the hearts of this generation to seek His face like never before. This eleventh hour outpouring is only the beginning until we see Him face to face. Press on dear saints and behold the Glory of the Lord.

Chapter 8

H-K

Hell

Experiencing visions or dreams of hell fall into one of two categories. First, it is often a call to the lost and dying in this world or to a people group. Second, it could be a gracious warning to turn to Christ, for the wages of sin is death, and the destiny of such is loss and eternal damnation (Matthew 10:28).

Homelessness

Seeing the homeless situations can range from having a call to the lost and homeless or intersession (James 1:27), to being a symbol of yours or someone else's spiritual condition. Spiritually, being homeless is a state of being lost, without a home in heaven, or a struggle with your old nature that is hindering your identity in Christ.

Seeing a bum for example, breaking into your house can speak to your old nature (flesh) raising its head and trying to tear down your life in the battlefield of the mind. Context and the tone of compassion will tell the tail.

Hygiene

Seeing symbolism related to one's hygiene often points to a condition in one's life. Symbolism in this category include things like:

Bad breath: Pointing to possibly something you have said that is negative or introspection and self-consciousness.

Bathing or washing: Symbolic of cleansing your life of something (Exodus 30:19-21).

Flushing: Speaks to discarding something in your life, including words aimed at you that may be negative or getting rid of an attribute or habit. John Wimber used to say, "*I always throw-out the bones when I eat chicken,*" good words to live by. Flushing can also refer to discarding wrong prophetic words in reference to creating a prophetic culture. The body should naturally flush words that miss the mark. This is a sign of a healthy and self-cleaning environment.

Using deodorant: Can symbolize covering up an offence in your life.

Intersession, Watching

Seeing yourself, others, or even angels watching over something is often symbolic of being an intercessor or a prophet, standing in the gap watching and protecting the walls of a person, ministry, community, or region (Isaiah 62:6; Jeremiah 6:17). An example of this might be seeing you standing on a hill, overlooking a valley with binoculars.

Keys

Keys are a very powerful symbol. More often than not they involve binding and loosing, as in Matthew 16:17-19 where the Lord says to Peter:

> *"Jesus answered and said to him, "Blessed are you, Simon Bar-Jonah, for flesh and blood has not revealed this to you, but My Father who is in heaven. And I also say to you that you are Peter, and on this rock I will build My church, and the gates of Hades shall not prevail against it. And I will give you the keys of the kingdom of heaven, and whatever you bind on earth will be bound in heaven, and what-*

> *ever you loose on earth will be loosed in heaven."*

The context of this message is clear; the keys of heaven bind the enemy, loose the captives, and release the resources of heaven to earth. We also see Jesus holding the keys of hades and death in Revelation 1:18. The context of that passage is Christ's divine authority of all creation, life, and death. The context of your dream or vision will drive its meaning. Keys may mean the following:

Authority: To bind the enemy or loose someone from bondage (a captive or prisoner). You may see a lock on shackles or a prison door, and know it is a word of knowledge to release an individual from bondage.

Access to a door that is locked: A locked door can mean that a.) The Lord is granting access, or b.) That he is closing the door.

Anointing: You may see golden keys falling from heaven like rain. Here the meaning is a release of fresh grace and anointing to carry out ministry and the opening of new areas of ministry.

Provision: You may see a treasure chest and keys used to unlock provision. Keys that release finance or resources are common.

Simplicity: You may have prayed for something personal like a new home or a car and God is giving you the keys to your quest. You may have simply lost your keys and in His grace, He is showing you where they are.

Chapter 9

L

Ladders, Steps, and Stairs

Often the Lord will use symbols that point to ascension, such as a ladder, a flight of stairs, climbing, taking steps, or ascending up an escalator (modern form of a ladder). I have often seen ladders in visions ascending into Heaven. At the heart of the revelation was God's call to climb higher, to press into His presence and seek that deeper place in Him. He wants us to press in to Him, to ascend to new levels of intimacy. Often this is the meaning of ascension symbols, but not always. In Genesis 28:12-13 we read where Jacob had a dream and in his dream he saw a ladder that stretched from earth to heaven and angels were ascending and descending on it. Listen to God's revelation regarding this dream.

> *"Also your descendants shall be as the dust of the earth; you shall spread abroad to the west and the east, to the north and the south; and in you and in your seed all the families of the earth shall be blessed. Behold, I am with you and will keep you wherever you go, and will bring you back to this land; for I will not leave you until I have done what I have spoken to you."*
>
> - Genesis 28:14-15

God did not mention angels though it is evident they were engaged in fulfilling the declaration of the Lord regarding Jacob and the nation. His dream was about the promise of inheritance and that his decedents would be vast and cover the earth, and that God would be with him and sustain him on his journey.

Always look at context, ask yourself what activity is happening. Am I climbing or descending? The answer to that will drive the context. Summary, ladders, steps, and stairs could mean the following:

- A call to you, your church, or others to climb higher and press into the presence of the Lord

- A word regarding promotion, that God is taking you to a higher place, spiritually or in your occupation

- A word regarding progression, such as "step out" "take the next step," or "move forward."

Land, Soil, Deserts, Valleys

Seeing the condition of land or some aspect of a landscape can be extremely powerful. Landscapes include deserts, valleys, mountains, remote areas, fields, sands and soils. They can speak to dryness, fruitfulness, kingdom glory, or strongholds. Obviously, the context points to its meaning. Here are a few examples:

Cold remote areas: Seeing regions that are cold and remote can symbolize feelings of being isolated and alone.

Islands: These can symbolize rest, isolation, or a temporary season of growth and development.

Fields: Fields, typically symbolize what God desires to do in your sphere of influence. Fields. Fields point to harvest. Conditions of a field usually have attached to them the solution to that condition. Of course, Jesus used the field to illustrate the heart of men and seeds sown in that heart (Matthew 13:31, seeds of faith; 13:38, 13:44, seeds of the enemy; seeds of salivation). Jesus also used the field as a symbol of the world (Matthew 13:36). Plowing a field can point to harvest or plowing the hard places of your heart, breaking up the follow ground.

Hills: Hills often speak of victory, triumph, or progression. Victory and progression call for the spirit of praise and thanksgiving (Psalm 98:8). Green hills speak to the fertilization of Christ's presence in your life and on your journey and walk with Him (Psalm 104:10-13).

Mountain (singular): Can speak to the mountain cut without hands (Daniel 2:45), our Savior and King, Jesus Christ. The mountain of the Lord is mighty and draws us into His presence (Exodus 19:18). The mountain of the Lord speaks not only of our desire to see Him and be with Him, but also speaks to our inheritance in Him as priests and kings of the Lord of Glory (Exodus 15:17). A mountain can also speak to a principality, problem, illness, or obstacle ready to be overtaken through faith and anointing in Christ (Mark 11:23; Psalm 125:1).

Pastures: Speak to the place of comfort, training, and nourishment to your soul. We are the sheep of His pasture, the sheep of His hand (Psalm 79:13, 95:7). We enter His gates and courts with praise and thanksgiving (Psalm 100:3).

Sands: Sands can speak to several things such as a house built on sand (pour foundation). Footprints in the sand (Jesus carrying you through a tough situation). Sands of time (speaking to the hour in which we live or your focus during this hour). Sands can speak to promise and generational blessing as in the case of Abraham. Quicksand can speak to a trap or snare of the enemy.

Tropical locations: Seeing peaceful tropical locations speak to a call to rest and relaxation.

Valley: Are often symbolic of low points in your life or a season of warfare where the Lord is pointing you to rest in the midst of battle (i.e. preparing a table for you in the presence of your enemy Psalm 23).

Wilderness: This includes deserts, dry, remote, or desolate places and often symbolizes a dry season in your life. Often this is a place of training and development. This can also speak to isolation in someone's life.

Light, Electricity, Lightning

Seeing light, lightening, lamps, lasers, and electricity, or the contrasts between light and darkness, can be very powerful, and often carry the message of power, illumination, or enlightenment. Here are a few examples:

Darkness: Darkness including gray scenes and shadowy places speaks to warfare and the power of Christ to overcome. It can include the word of promise of intercession.

Flashlights or Search Lights: This category of lighting refers to finding one's way in the dark or illuminating a safe harbor for those lost in the dark (Psalm 18:28). It can also symbolize the study of His Word (Psalm 119:105).

Lamps, Lanterns, & Light Bulbs: This category is much like the previous, but may also carry the idea of God's protection and an increase in His anointing (Psalm 132:17). Lamps also speak to your walk with Christ and being filled with the Holy Spirit (Matthew 5:15, 6:22; Luke 11:33).

Lasers: Lasers, like the latter, speak to the power of His Word and the power of proclamation. Lasers cut away and pierce throw the impossible with pointed accuracy.

Light, Highlights, & Illumination: Seeing light, highlights, or illumination on people is often a gift of discernment. It is the ability to see what God is doing, or about to do, for someone. This can come through the gift or prophecy or a word of knowledge. Often the colors associated with light can point to a call or activity that God is doing. Of course, Jesus is the light of the world and His presence illuminates our lives and our path. The Holy Spirit will illuminate us with revelation and knowledge in Him.

Lightning & Electricity: Symbolizes the power of the Holy Spirit for renewal, healing, etc. The rain of God coming with power and glory that shakes a region. Lightning also speaks to proclamation and the prophetic (Job 37:3). Impartation of gifting and release of the Holy Spirit can also be symbolized through seeing an electrical current or lightening.

Light Shows: Lightshows in the heavens such as aurora speak to the glory and majesty of Him who sits upon the throne. See the chapter on Aurora in part one.

Chapter 10

M

Medical, Sickness, Healing

Visionary symbols involving sickness are often literal words of knowledge regarding something the Lord want's to heal. Remember, what the Lord reveals, He heals. There are two exceptions to this. The first typically takes place in a dream and is symbolic of something in your personal life, either emotional or spiritual. The second is a word of knowledge regarding another person that is metaphorical, a vision that points to a spiritual or emotional condition. Examples include:

Band Aids: Speak to covering up a wound or hurt in your life that is temporary or you are hiding it and the Lord wants to uncover it and bring healing to the situation.

Broken Bones: Often broken bones can be symbolic of having a broken place in your life. A broken arm can speak to powerlessness. A broken rib can speak to a broken relationship. A broken foot can speak to something in your life that is affecting your walk with Christ. A broken hip can speak to trial and wrestling with God. A broken finger can symbolize accusation or something spoken that is judgmental.

Bruises: Often speaks to emotional trauma or something from you past that needs of healing.

Coma: This can speak of depression or spiritual stupor. It may involve spiritual warfare or demonic oppression.

Chocking: This can speak to a spiritual attack or something trying to cut off your voice. This can also speak to an inability to listen, something that is hard to swallow.

Scars: Often speaks to past hurts or curses in one's life and points to a need for healing.

Surgery: Usually points to a work the Holy Spirit is doing in someone's life.

Metal

Seeing metal can be symbolic of an attribute or insight into something. For example, bronze can speak to the strength of the Lord, while Iron on the other hand speaks to the strength of men. Gold speaks to the glory of God and His kingdom or the richness of His ministry in your life.

Fool's gold speaks to a lie or false religion or doctrine. Silver speaks to redemption, or the purity of a ministry and Christ in your life, or the power of His Word. Tin, speaks to worthlessness, cheapness, or something of little value in the kingdom.

Mirrors, Pictures

Looking in a mirror can speak to reflection, identity, self-image, vanity, or a memory of the past. Self-identity is powerful and can launch you into your future or hinder your destiny with false identity. A healthy identity sees one's self in Christ and seated at the right hand of Holy royalty, subservient to the King and His glorious Kingdom.

A poor identity can be linked to past wounds, poor self-esteem, or believing the lies of the enemy. God's desire for you is that of son-ship and royalty. You have been bought for a price and have been grafted into the heavenly family. The most cross life is a life of victory and love. It is a life of access and He has opened the windows of heaven over you.

Pictures can speak to your past or to a person in need of prayers and intersession. If God shows you a portrait of yourself and it is, glorious he is calling forth your identity in Him and wants you to see how He sees you. If you see a picture of yourself that is distorted, this is symbolic of a poor self-image. Pictures of people can also be a word of knowledge that God is giving you regarding someone.

Music and Worship

David made this proclamation:

"Praise the Lord with the harp; Make melody to Him with an instrument of ten strings. Sing to Him a new song; Play skillfully with a shout of joy. For the word of the Lord is right, and all His work is done in truth. He loves righteousness and justice; the earth is full of the goodness of the Lord."

- Psalm 33:2-5

Experiencing music and worship in a dream or vision often speaks to joy, celebration, thanksgiving, victory, and breakthrough. Worldly music, on the other hand, can point to being in a situation or atmosphere that is unhealthy or a bad environment. Individual instruments or melodies can speak to a worship or prophetic call. Here are a few examples:

Bell: Bells often speak to a call to missions or to power evangelism. A mission bell is a good example of this.

Flutes: A flute can speak to your walk with God. The melody can speak to a wooing, a loving call to follow.

Stringed Instruments: Melodies on stringed instruments such as a guitar can be a call to the ministry of worship. This can include prophetic proclamation through song.

Trumpets and Horns: Carry a sense of urgency, a call to attention, or a call to proclaim a prophetic word from the Lord. Many times the Lord will alter the focus or direction of a ministry or person, giving a declarative call to do something. Horns also speak to power and strength in Christ. Trumpets can speak to a call to warfare or taking a warfare stance.

Melodies: Depending on the song can speak to the Holy Spirit or Christ's tender embrace and a healing work of love He is doing in your life.

Chapter 11

N

Numbers

Numbers, like colors, often carry meaning. The Scriptures are full of numeric patterns that speak to various truths. Numbers can be literal, but also carry a meaning that is personally significant to you. E.W. Bullinger in his classic work "Numbers in Scripture" (first published in 1894) writes on this topic extensively. Here are a few examples:

One: the number one represents unity, oneness, and God (Deuteronomy 6:4).

Two: Is the symbol of witness (Mark 6:7), testimony (Matthew 18:19), unity (Matthew 19:5), or choice (as in choose between two – Matthew 6:24).

Three: Speaks to the Godhead, Father, Son, and Holy Spirit. It can also represent completeness, fullness, or perfection (Ephesians 3:19, 4:13; Colossians 2:9).

Four: Speaks to things created Genesis 1:14-19), established boundaries, or realms of authority (4 seasons; 4 regions of the earth – north, south, east, and west; 4 corners; 4 sides; a cube being 4 x 4; 4 elements – earth, air, fire, and water). Four living creatures surround His throne (Revelation 4:6-8). The bride of Christ symbolized as the New Jerusalem is symbolized as a square or cube coming out of heaven (Revelation 21:9-21).

Five: Is symbolic of favor, blessing, and grace. The five smooth stones of David, speak of God's grace to defeat Goliath. This is also seen in Leviticus 26:8 where five will chase a hundred. Five also speaks to the hand of God, as in the last two examples. Other examples of five speaking to grace include anointing oil which had have parts (Exodus 30:23-25) and incense, representing the prayers of the saints, was made of five parts (Exodus 30:34). The Hebrew word for "gift" appears five times in the Old Testament. The Greek word "Parakleetos" translated "comforter" (speaking of the Holy Spirit) appears five times in the New Testament (4 in John – 14:16, 26, 15:26, 16:7 and once in 1 John 2:1). There are five office gifts of Christ listed in Ephesians 4:7-16.

Six: Is symbolic of man or humanity. Man was created on the sixth day (Genesis 1:31). Six also speaks to human labor or the work of one's hands (Exodus 6:22). Six can also symbolizes man's imperfection and lost dominion. The sixth commandment relates to the worst sin – murder. Six can symbolize false accusation – Christ was accused of having a demon six times in the gospels (Mark 3:22; John 7:20; 8:48, 52; 10:20; Luke 11:15). This act confirms man's enmity with the person of Jesus Christ. In the book of Nehemiah, we see six-fold opposition to the work of God (2:10; 2:19; 4:1-4, 7, 8; 6:1, 2, 7, 9-14). Words that appear only six times in scripture include destruction (Hebrew: avaddohn), yoke (Hebrew: moht), shame (Greek: aischunee), to change (Greek: allatte), ungodliness (Greek: asebeia), or abomination (Greek: bdelugma). The first miracle in the book of John was changing water to wine in six earthen vessels, speaking to the healing and redemption of man and filling the earthly vessel with the Spirit of the living God (John 2).

Seven: In scripture seven is symbolic of spiritual perfection or completion. In Isaiah 11:2 we see the seven Spirits of God marking Christ. In Joel 2:28, 29, we see the Holy Spirit poured out on seven people groups. The golden candlestick had six branches and one steam making seven points of light. The armor of God in Ephesians 6:14-18 consists of seven parts, the latter being prayer. In Hebrew, the root word for seven is "savah" meaning to be full or satisfied, to have enough of. Of course, on the seventh day of creation God rested, giving us the Sabbath.

Abraham receive a seven-fold blessing from God in Genesis 7:2, 3. In Judges 6, there are seven attributes listed as qualifications for service. Jesus preformed seven miracles in the book of John. He spoke seven words to the woman of Samaria. During His life on earth He had seven appearances of angels. Of course there are seven letters to seven churches in the book of Revelation. We also see seven seals and seven trumpets. In Matthew 13 Jesus gave seven parables. There are seven "gifts" in Romans 7, "unities" in Ephesians 4, "characteristics of wisdom" in James 3, "gifts of Christ" in John's gospel, "better things" in Hebrews, "titles of Christ" in Hebrews. Clean beasts were taken into the ark by sevens. Finely, the mystery of God is completed in the seventh vial of the seventh trumpet of the seventh seal in the book of Revelation. The number seven is stamped throughout the scripture.

Eight: The number eight in Hebrew is the word "Sh'moneh" from the root "Shah'meyn" meaning to "to make fat", "cover with fat", "to super-abound". It carries the meaning of a "superabundant" life or "fertile". Eight is also the number of "new beginnings". It is the number of resurrection and regeneration.

Other than the Lord and the saints, there are eight resurrection in scriptures (3 in the Old Testament, 3 in the Gospels, 2 in the book of Acts). The feast of Tabernacles lasted 8 days (John 1:14). The transfiguration of Jesus took place on the 8th day. There are 8 songs in the Old

Testament outside the Psalms. Elijah preformed 8 miracles in Kings. Elisha preformed double that number (14). There are 8 references to the Old Testament in Revelation 1.

In my own life 8 symbolizes "new beginnings." My daughter was born at 8:08 in 88. Every time I see the number 808 I am reminded of His complete control to fulfill all of His promises and dreams in my life. It is established like bookends (808). When I see 818, the Lord speaks to my heart about being one-step closer and His continued hand on my life.

Nine: The number nine in Scripture is the number of judgment. There were 27 sieges of Jerusalem (3 x 9), 3 symbolizing God's completeness, and 9 being the number of judgment. The judgments of God in Haggai contain 9 components (Haggai 1:11). Words that occur 9 times in the New Testament include bottomless pit, or deep; ungodly, lasciviousness, and lightning. From a redemptive standpoint, there are 9 gifts of the Holy Spirit in 1 Corinthians 12:8-10. These gifts are given to produce life and bring redemption, a model of the churches role in judging: under the New Convenient, we bless and curse not!

Ten: This is the number of completeness and represents law and divine order, or nations. It can also represent God's portion, i.e. tithe. We see completeness in Noah as being the 10th generation from Adam; the 10 commandments; the tithe; the 10 plagues of Egypt in Exodus; the 10 worldly kingdoms of antichrist; the 10 nations of Genesis 15:19; the ten trials of Abraham's faith; and the 10 rebellions of Israel in the wilderness (Numbers 14:22).

Ten times in the Old Testament, fire fell from heaven, six of which were judgments. We also see shouts of Joy mentioned ten times in the Old Testament. We have the parable of the ten virgins. Ten times the phrase, "I have sinned" mentioned in scripture. There are ten parables of the kingdom in the gospel of Matthew. Ten times Jesus uses the phrase "I AM" in the book of John, pointing to the voice in the burning bush, "tell them I AM has sent you" and for this they tried to stone Him.

Eleven: This number is marked by disorder, disorganization, or imperfection. This is seen in the 11 sons of Jacob and the lives of Jehoiakim and Zedekiah who both reigned for 11 years. Of course, we have the phrase "11th hour" in Matthew 20: 6, 9, speaking to the time of the end and an accounting of one's work and wages.

Twelve: This number symbolizes Divine government as seen in the 12 tribes of Israel; the 12 Apostles; and the 24 elders before the throne in the book of Revelation (12 x 2). We also see 12 foundations in the heavenly Jerusalem with 12 gates, 12 pearls, and 12 angels. Its measurement was 12,000 furlongs square (144 or 12 x 12 cubits). 12 people were anointed in the Old Testament. Jesus was 12 years old when He first appeared in public. 12 legions of angels are mentioned in Matthew

26:53. The day is divided into 2 – 12 hour parts (night 12 hours, day 12 hours). There are 12 months in a year.

Numeric perfection

Numeric perfection is everywhere. We not only see it in scripture but also in the mater created by the author of scripture, God. In his 1894 in his Christian classic "Numbers in Scripture," E. W. Bullinger points out some fascinating facts. Consider nature, with numeric stamps marked throughout. Take the rows of kernel-corn on a cob of Indian corn. Wither straight or spiral they are always arranged in even numbers, never odd.

When we look at the leaves on a plant, we notice that they always grow in a spiral and as they spiral, after a certain number of leaves, one leaf will always line up with the first leaf, creating a numeric pattern. In the case of the apple it lines up at the fifth leaf; the oak is the forth, the peach is the sixth; and the holly it is the eighth, and in the case of the holly, it takes two turns before lining up.

This numeric pattern is woven into to everything. In physiology, there are seven divisions of age: Infancy, childhood, youth, adolescence, manhood, decline, and senility. We also see this numeric thumb print of the Holy Spirit on the development of life. Consider gestation periods, which are often marked by the number seven, wither days or weeks. The mouse is 21 days (3 x 7), hare and rat is 28 days (4 x 7), cat is 56 days (8 x 7), dog is 63 days (9 x 7), lion is 98 days (14 x 7), sheep is 147 days (21 x 7), a hen is 21 days (3 x 7), a duck is 28 days (4 x 7) and the human is 280 days (40 x 7).

This numeric perfection extends to every created being as well. Take the bee for example. The number 3 marks the bee. In 3 days the egg is hatched. It is fed for 9 days and reaches maturity in 15 days. The worker bee reaches maturity in 21 days and it works for 3 days after leaving its cell. The bee is composed of three parts, the head and two stomachs. The eyes are made up of 3,000 small eyes. The bee has 6 legs composed of three parts. The foot has 3 sections and the antennae consist of nine sections. Is this by chance? I do not think so. It is the beauty of design by an incredibly loving creator.

In music and sound, we see the same perfection as seen in the seven notes or tones in a music scale. Light or electromagnetic radiation is classified into eight classes, seven not visible and one visible to the human eye:

- Gamma radiation
- X-ray radiation
- Ultraviolet radiation
- Visible radiation (Color)
- Infrared radiation

- Terahertz radiation

- Microwave radiation

- Radio waves

The visible spectrum of light (color), according to Newton, consists of seven primary colors, as seen in the color spectrum of a rainbow or in the breaking of white light through a prism. Color (vibration of light) and sound (vibration of air) both are divided into two groups: three primary and four secondary, from which all others proceed.

For the purpose of this section of the book regarding numeric symbolism, it is very clear that the Lord uses numeric symbols when speaking to us through the language of visions and dreams.

There are many other examples of numeric symbolism in scripture than those listed. Here are a few more with brief explanations.

Twenty Four: an elder in the Church or elderly wisdom (Revelation 4:10)

Forty: judgment (Genesis 7:4); wilderness experience or a season of wondering (Exodus 16:35, Deuteronomy 2:7, Joshua 5:6); season of rest (Judges 3:11. 5:31, 8:28); or a time of warfare perpetration (Matthew 4:2).

Fifty: Grace, Jubilee or free from debt (Leviticus 25:10)

Seventy: Elders (Exodus 24:9); A full life (Psalm 23:15); Season of judgment or set seasonal framework (Jeremiah 25:11-12; Daniel 9:24); Grace as seen in forgiveness (Matthew 18:22). Being sent or ministry expansion (Luke 10:1-2).

Eighty: Extended grace (Psalm 90:10)

One Hundred: Blessings and the fruit of ministry or one's life (Mark 4:8).

One Hundred Fifty Three: Revival and great harvest (John 21:11).

Six Hundred Sixty Six: End times and the beast, the man of sin, the antichrist (666).

CHAPTER 12

O-P

Occult and Witchcraft

Any symbolism involving the occult speaks to demonic activity and influences. This includes tarot cards, palm reading, Ouija boards, fortune telling, witchcraft, zodiac signs, séances, etc. If an animal, person, or supernatural being manifests it and speaks to you and the essence of the dialog relates to a spirit guide, this is demonic. Often a demon will pose as guide, and even can come at times as a relative.

The scripture is very clear in this matter (Deuteronomy 18:10; Leviticus 20:6; 2 Kings 9:22; Acts 16:16; Ezekiel 21:21). If you are harassed by the demonic, resist the devil and he will flee. Seek spirit-filled counsel and prayer. If you have been involved in the occult repentance and reconciliation is essential.

Oil

Oil most always symbolizes an outpouring of the Holy Spirit, renewal, or anointing including not just anointing for service but also healing. Oil is often seen as golden. However, it may be black like crude oil, which speaks to the heritage of the saints and the release of rich blessing that fuels and energizes the body of Christ.

Oil may appear in many types of vessels including lamps, buckets, falling as in rain, or bubbling up like crude from the ground. The vessel and quantity of oil may have meaning as well. Is God pouring out the oil? Are you personally carrying a lamp with oil? Are you anointing someone with oil? Each of these will carry their tone of meaning. Context will determine what God is saying. See Matthew 25:1-10, Psalm 23:5, 45:7.

Plant Life

Plants speak of life, wither vibrant and growing or withered, dry and dying. Plants are dependent; they need three things to grow and thrive: water, sunlight, and healthy soil. The energy of the sun transforms air (carbon dioxide) into sugar. We call this photosynthesis. Water brings life and structure to the plants, and soil imparts nutrients for healthy cell function.

Symbolically, this is evident, we have the life changing power and radiant light of the Son of God transforming the very air we breathe, giving us the Holy Spirit like wind from heaven, and pouring in us living water, that we may thrive and grow into His image and nature. He transforms the very soil of our hearts so that we can draw upon the nutrients of heaven. Without basting in His presence and being watered by His Word, we wither. Without good soil (Matthew 13:8), the Word cannot take root and growth, life and fruitfulness is hindered. All plants have some type of root system. Visually seeing a root system most always points to a symptom of something. Jesus explained this very clearly in the parable of the sower.

> *"Then He spoke many things to them in parables, saying: 'Behold, a sower went out to sow. And as he sowed, some seed fell by the wayside; and the birds came and devoured them. Some fell on stony places, where they did not have much earth; and they immediately sprang up because they had no depth of earth.*
>
> *But when the sun was up they were scorched, and because they had no root they withered away. And some fell among thorns, and the thorns sprang up and choked them. But others fell on good ground and yielded a crop: some a hundredfold, some sixty, some thirty. He who has ears to hear, let him hear.'"*

- Matthew 13:3-9

He goes on to explain the meaning in verses 18 to 23:

> *"Therefore hear the parable of the sower: When anyone hears the word of the kingdom, and does not understand it, then the wicked one comes and snatches away what was sown in his heart. This is he who received seed by the wayside. But he who received the seed on stony places, this is he who hears the word and immediately receives it with joy; yet he has no root in himself, but endures only for a while. For when tribulation or persecution arises because of the word, immediately he stumbles. Now he who received seed among the thorns is he who hears the word, and the cares of this world and the deceitfulness of riches choke the word, and he becomes unfruitful. But he who received seed on the good ground is he who hears the word and understands it, who indeed bears fruit and produces: some a hundredfold, some sixty, some thirty."*

Root systems are powerful. They point to things that hinder us in our walk with Christ. We see roots of bitterness (Hebrews 12:5), roots of lust or greed (1 Timothy 6:10), roots of rebellion (Isaiah 5:24), roots of promise (Isaiah 37:31), or roots of inheritance and blessing (Romans 11:16-18; 15:12). When God shows us a root system, it is often a word of knowledge pointing to His desire to heal an area of one's life. Sometimes that means laying an ax to the root of the tree or uprooting something in the heart or mind. Sometimes healing comes through saturating our hearts with living water by soaking in His presence.

Plant symbolism takes many forms and not only includes the plant type and its condition, but also may include the landscape, scene, season, or action (i.e. farming, planting, surveying, and watering). Here are a few examples of plants and their meaning (for symbolism relating to fruit – see fruit; trees – see trees).

Flowers: Flowers speak to love, harmony, and fruitfulness. They call out the glory of what God is doing or bringing forth in one's life. They carry the aroma of Heaven and draw people into His presence.

Gardens: Gardens speak to the work of God in your life relating to your walk, mind, or ministry. A garden is about fertility and expansion. Gardens are kept and pruned by the master gardener, the Holy Spirit.

Grass: Speaks to green pastures, comfort, and grazing. Grass carries in it peace and tranquility, or being called to a place of rest.

Herbs: Speak to the love gifts of the Father, those natural gifting He pours into the life of all people. They are not only fragrant but also edible and are used to round out the make-up of a person or group. When one honors the gifting of the Father in one's life it spawns wholeness to the individual and the culture.

Leaves: Speak to growth, transition, or change. Green leaves blowing in the wind can speak to a season of growth in the Holy Spirit. Autumn leaves speak of transition between the seasons of your life. Withered leaves speak to dry areas of one's life and the need for living water.

Lily Pads: The water lily speaks to navigation, as in how to navigate the waters of life in Christ. As a water plant, their source of life comes from the water. Typically, you will see lily pads scattered across a pound or stream like steppingstones.

Reeds: Reeds or water-grass speaks to wading in the presence of God. They speak to the understanding of your metron and line the boundaries of your life. Reeds gain their life substance from the river and thrive at the water's edge.

Seeds: Speak to planting and birthing. Seed in the Greek is "sperma," meaning that which is sown. It is the germ of life. It speaks to heritage, linage, family, offspring, or ministry. Sometimes it speaks residue or remnant - that which is left - and out of a few many shall grow. Seeds can also speak to faith and promise.

Sprouts or Shoots: Sprouts speak to that which is shooting forth, growth, springing up or budding. This is an action word that points to something springing up or being brought forth. Sprouts also speak to the "newness" of something - its tenderness and fragility. Sprouts need care to become strong.

Thorns: A thorn bush speaks to possible danger either in life-style choices or in actions.

> *"By their fruit you will recognize them. Do people pick grapes from thorn bushes, or figs from thistles?"*
>
> – Matthew 7:16.

They gave Jesus a crown of thorns. Jesus spoke of seed sown amongst thorns (Matthew 13:7).

Vines: A vine is symbolic of Christ and His church. A vine can also speak of a person's life or their relationship to the church. A grape vine or vineyard speaks to the fruit of God's grace upon His people, the nectar of heaven released into the earth.

Weeds: Weeds speak of falsehood or lies. They grow up to choke out the truth. They hinder the growth of harvest. Weeds can also speak to the lost or the sons of the evil one. At the end of the ages, the reapers will gather the weeds and cast them into the fire. Thorns and weeds often grow together. Weeds take over the fruit of labor and choke out provision.

Chapter 13

Q-R

Roads, Trails & Potholes

Roads, trails, or paths often speak to our walk with Christ in this life. Sometimes the road involves a decision we have to make, other times it points to our progress or regress. Are their obstacles in the road? Is the road straight and smooth or rugged, rocky, and full of potholes? Is the path progressing down a hill or up a mountain? Can you see the distance or is there a bind up ahead? Life choices often are symbolized on a road. If it is bumpy and hard, it could symbolize a rough season in life. If it is smooth, it may be highlighting God's favor upon your life and walk.

Pay attention to the condition of the road or the way the road engages the landscape. Things like roadside signage, bridges, tunnels, rocks, potholes, fallen trees, and such each carry a meaning. God may be igniting hope or faith in your life or He may be bringing a warning or showing you a change in direction.

Rocks, Walls

A rock in general is symbolic of Christ and can speak of Christ as your refuge and strength. At the same time, a rock can speak to the condition or your heart i.e. stony heart. Context will always tell the story. Stony walls on the other hand speak of an obstacle. If a stone wall is incomplete or falling down it could speak of something that needs to be rebuilt. Alternatively, it might point to rebuilding the defenses in your life and putting on the full armor of God.

Walls are interesting. On the one hand, they can symbolize a boundary embossed by God, or a hindrance put up by the enemy, such as barbed wire. God also puts up a hedge of protection around us; we can see this as an actual hedge or a wall as in a fortress. Hiding behind a wall can mean finding protection, being in a state of fear, or being bound by a past hurt.

Royalty

God so desires you to understand your place in the kingdom. As a child of God, you are of the royal line of heaven. You are kings and priests of the Lord. Having a healthy understanding of your identity in Christ produce fruit and a mindset that is able to flow with His Spirit in your life and ministry. Peter tells us in 1 Peter 2:9, 10 that,

> *"... You are a chosen generation, a royal priesthood, a holy nation, His own special people, that you may proclaim the praises of Him who called you out of darkness into His marvelous light; who once were not a people but are now the people of God, who had not obtained mercy but now have obtained mercy."*

Symbolisms of royalty include crowns, scepters, the throne room, signet rings, a staff, a royal garment, or being a prince in a kingdom. Embrace you position in Christ and move out as an ambassador of heaven.

Running

Running in a dream can symbolize a few things. If you are running in a race it speak to your walk of ministry in Christ and God is encouraging you to press on and run the race as if to win (Philippians 2:16). He longs for you to obtain the victor's crown and cheers you on, pointing you into the way to go. Jogging can speak to a healthy pace in your walk with Christ.

Running away from something speaks to fear and being chased by the enemy or by a stumbling block. Supernatural running like outrunning a car or motorcycle speaks to divine acceleration and progression in your ministry life. God is showing you your progression and success and is encouraging you press on in His power and might.

Chapter 14

S

Seas, Lakes, Rivers, and Streams

There is probably no other symbol greater in scripture regarding the grace, peace, and presence of Christ and the Holy Spirit than rivers, streams, waterfalls, fountains, and water. We see the power of the river symbol in Ezekiel's famous vision in chapter 47 verses 1-12, where the river of God flows out of the temple in all directions, and on its banks grow fruit whose leaves bring healing.

> *"Then he brought me back to the door of the temple; and there was water, flowing from under the threshold of the temple toward the east, for the front of the temple faced east; the water was flowing from under the right side of the temple, south of the altar. He brought me out by way of the north gate, and led me*

around on the outside to the outer gateway that faces east; and there was water, running out on the right side.

And when the man went out to the east with the line in his hand, he measured one thousand cubits, and he brought me through the waters; the water came up to my ankles. Again he measured one thousand and brought me through the waters; the water came up to my knees. Again he measured one thousand and brought me through; the water came up to my waist. Again he measured one thousand, and it was a river that I could not cross; for the water was too deep, water in which one must swim, a river that could not be crossed. He said to me, "Son of man, have you seen this?" Then he brought me and returned me to the bank of the river.

When I returned, there, along the bank of the river, were very many trees on one side and the other. Then he said to me: "This water flows toward the eastern region, goes down into the valley, and enters the sea. When it reaches the sea, its waters are healed. And it shall be that every living thing that moves, wherever the rivers go, will live. There will be a very great multitude of fish, because these waters go there; for they will be healed, and everything will live wherever the river goes. It shall be that fishermen will stand by it from En Gedi to En Eglaim; they will be places for spreading their nets. Their fish will be of the

> same kinds as the fish of the Great Sea, exceedingly many. But its swamps and marshes will not be healed; they will be given over to salt. Along the bank of the river, on this side and that, will grow all kinds of trees used for food; their leaves will not wither, and their fruit will not fail. They will bear fruit every month, because their water flows from the sanctuary. Their fruit will be for food, and their leaves for medicine."

Zechariah tells us that on the day Christ returns, His feet will land on the Mount of Olives and split it from east to west and out of the mouth of that split will flow a river of living-water. John sees the river of the water of life in Revelation 22, and like Ezekiel, the leaves of the fruit trees bring healing to the nations. Jeremiah refers to God as the fountain of living water. Jesus said:

> "If you knew the gift of God and who it is that asks you for a drink, you would have asked him and he would have given you living water.
>
> Sir, the woman said, you have nothing to draw with and the well is deep. Where can you get this living water? Are you greater than our father Jacob, who gave us the well and drank from it himself, as did also his sons and his livestock?
>
> Jesus answered, Everyone who drinks this water will be thirsty again, but whoever

> *drinks the water I give them will never thirst. Indeed, the water I give them will become in them a spring of water welling up to eternal life."*

- John 4:10-14

And again,

> *"On the last and greatest day of the festival, Jesus stood and said in a loud voice, let anyone who is thirsty come to me and drink. Whoever believes in me, as Scripture has said, rivers of living water will flow from within them."*

- John 7:37, 38

The mood, tone, scene, and action, taking place while seeing rivers, streams, waterfalls, and such help determine the voice of Christ. If the river is raging it may speak to turmoil blocking your ability to press into Him. If a river is full of life and you can see fish, swimming about it speaks to abundance and revival. If you are peering into the water and you see it bubbling it is symbolic of the prophetic and wisdom being released. If you find yourself stepping into the water and you are moving from shallow to deep, it is symbolic of your progressing and God's call to bring you deeper in Him.

Oceans are often symbolic of the nations. Calming stormy seas is symbolic of intersession. Seeing Christ calming the seas is symbolic for His deep love for the nations or for you. A tidal wave can be symbolic of revival coming or it may be impending disaster. If you are in a boat on the ocean, it can refer to your life, walk, or ministry in Christ.

Seasons

Seasons usually symbolize times, epochs, periods, stages, or chapters in your life or the life of the church or people group. In the ancient times of the Hebrew people, seasons spoke of and centered on the harvest. The very lives of the people, as an agrarian society, were dependent upon the harvest. In life we move through periods that reflect the nature of the seasons. There is a time for everything under the sun and seasons speak to those times. Here are a few examples:

> *"And it shall be that if you earnestly obey My commandments which I command you today, to love the Lord your God and serve Him with all your heart and with all your soul, then I will give you the rain for your land in its season, the early rain and the latter rain, that you may gather in your grain, your new wine, and your oil. And I will send grass in your fields for your livestock that you may eat and be filled."*
>
> - Deuteronomy 11:13-15

> *"Preach the word! Be ready in season and out of season."*
>
> - 2 Timothy 4:2

Autumn: Speaks of transition, the end of a season, completion, change, harvest, reflection, rejoicing, or time of preparation.

Spring: Speaks to the newness of life, new beginnings, life, harvest, renewal, refreshing, regeneration and salvation.

Summer: Speaks to opportunity, trial, community, fellowship, vacation, service, heat of affliction, or preparation.

Winter: Speaks to rest, tranquility, going deeper in Christ, strength, heritage, remembering the accomplishments of God in your life, dormant, or waiting on God.

Sight, Eyes, and Lens

Symbols relating to your ability to see most always speak to your ability to see as God sees or from His perspective. For example, if you are wearing glasses, God is giving you wisdom to see clearly and go deeper. If your lenses are colored it could mean that you are filtering what you are seeing and God is calling you to look from a different perspective. If you lens are dirty there is something hindering you from seeing clearly. This could be sin or a belief system. Likewise, windows carry the same meaning a lens.

If you are blindfolded it is symbolic of having a blockage to see the truth. If you are blind, it is symbolic of the need for salvation or repentance that you may see and know the truth, Christ Jesus.

If you see your eyes, God is showing you that you have the eyes of a Seer. Wide eyes mean He is expanding your ability to see. Binoculars speak to seeing beyond you current situation, gaining understanding or being prophetic.

Signs, Banners, and Billboards

Signs, banners, and billboards always carry a message God is trying to get across to you. Here are a few examples and their possible meaning:

Banners: Usually speak to victory in your life and God's favor over you. Banners are a call to celebrate.

Billboards: Are important messages to get your attention. They are large and typically, on the side of the road speaking to the direction you are heading.

Bumper Stickers: Speak to a belief or life message that is important to you in your life.

Direction Signs: Speak to point you in the right direction. They are markers to guide you. Street signs speak to the same thing.

Exit Sign: Speaks to a way out of a situation.

Hazard Sign: Is a warning to be cautious and avert an upcoming hazard.

Mile Markers: Speak to progression and your growth in your life.

Stop Signs: Are symbolic to stop, reflect, look in all directions, and only proceed when you have the right of way or a green light from the Lord.

Yield Sign: Is symbolic of submitting to authority or your need to be humble.

Sounds

Sounds often have meaning in dreams or visions. They can symbolize warnings, proclamations, messages, or worship. Here are a few examples:

Amplifier: Is symbolic of a message going out and the call to speak and proclaim.

Barking: Is symbolic of a spiritual enemy coming against you trying to intimidate you.

Chatter: Is symbolic of the cares of a people group and the call to intersession. On the negative side, it could symbolize confusion and a call to be still and listen in a season of rest.

Crying: Is symbolic of the crying of a people and God calling you to act on their behalf.

Echo: Is symbolic of the sound of salvation going across the land, His word not returning void.

Music: The call to worship and go deep into the love of Christ.

Sirens and Alarms: Are symbolic of warning, a call to be alert or awaken to do something.

Soft Stringed Instrument: A call to rest in the love of God or to soak in His presence.

Trumpets: The call to proclaim a message from the Lord, to herald, or gather the people of God.

Whispers: Hearing the secret thing of Christ or on the negative side, gossip.

Space

Symbolism relating to things in space such as planets, stars, and space speak to the glory of God and His bigness. He uses symbols like this to call you into your destiny. He is pointing to things bigger than you are. He is expanding your vision and giving you promise. Seeing the sun points to Christ and His power and burning love for you.

Speaking

Symbolism relating to speech speak either to the conduct of your actions or the call to speak and proclaim. Belching or burping speaks to wrong things coming out of your mouth. A bridle speaks to the same thing but also speaks to a lack of self-control. Biting someone is symbolic of strife or fighting with someone.

On the other hand, speaking through a microphone is a call to proclaim to a people group. Whistling speaks to supporting or calling someone to Christ. Speaking in a foreign language is a call to a people group or speaking so that others understand what you are saying.

Sports & Games

Sports and games are powerful symbolic language of God, the former speaking to position and destiny, the later speaking to strategies for victory. In sports related symbols the position you play is just as important as the game itself. In games, it is all about making the right move. Most often, the thrust of sport symbolism is a call to participate and win. Sport metaphors are loaded with promise and hope for your future. They reach out and call you to get with the program and take it to the finish line. Games are solo; sports are about your importance on the team. Here are a few examples:

Baseball: It is the ninth inning, bases are loaded, and you are up at bat. It is not too late for you. You were made for this hour. The team is depending on you and it is your time, you are not too old to get back in the game. It is not too late. If you step up and swing… the team wins. Now is your time. Seize the day and take your place in His story. Think "the Natural", or "Field of Dreams." Are you on the bench or in the game?

Basketball: All sports are about teamwork, but I think basketball illustrates the beauty of teamwork and precision like no other. There is finesse in basketball. In basketball, everyone has to learn to dribble, shoot, and maneuver. Without the team fully engaged, there is no win. The big question is, Are you a team player, fully equipped to take the shot at any given moment?

Cards: Many people live their lives from a position of stagnancy. They view their situation as if they were stuck. They feel as if they must live their life with the cards they were dealt, not knowing that God can win with any hand. When we walk through life with the eyes of faith, we believe in destiny. We dream the impossible and those impossible dreams become our future.

Cheerleading: Cheerleading is all about the gift of encouragement. Like Barnabas was to Paul, this gift lifts up those around them with a voice of victory. Their ministry is that of enablement. They are partners in ministry holding up the right hand and the left. They are like the cloud of witnesses that cheer on the saints to victory.

Chess: Chess is a game of strategy. Seeing yourself playing chess is God's promise to give you clarity and wisdom in dealing with a situation. He wants to show you how to navigate your steps in such a way as if to win.

Football: Football is about taking ground across enemy lines and brings the ball to the end zone. Football is warfare. George Carlen said it well: "In football the object is for the quarterback, also known as the field general, to be on target with his aerial assault, riddling the defense by hitting his receivers with deadly accuracy in spite of the blitz, even if he has to use shotgun. With short bullet passes and long bombs, he marches his troops into enemy territory, balancing this aerial assault with a sustained ground attack that punches holes in the forward wall of the enemy's defensive line. In baseball, the object is to go home! And to be safe! - I hope I'll be safe at home!"

The metaphor is obvious, the question is: Are you in the game? God is a God of promise and destiny and He speaks to draw you into the game. He wants to throw you the long bomb. He wants you to run, block, kick, and fight your way into the enemy lines and win. What position are you playing?

Gambling: In Christ, there is no gamble. Seeing yourself gambling points to things in your life that erode your faith. In essence, you are gambling with your future. God's desire for you is to hear the voice of heaven and to run the race through faith. Life in Christ is not a game of chance.

Gymnastics, Ballet: When I think of gymnastics and ballet I think of beauty and grace comingled with strength. I call this symbolism the dance of the Bride where the grace of God shines forth in power and beauty. This is a picture of the end times Bride in all her glory.

Hiking & Rock Climbing: This type of symbolism is about staying the course. It is about ascension and God is calling you to press onward and upward and to obtain the high calling of your Lord.

Hockey: When I think of hockey, I usually think of a goalkeeper. He is the one guy on the ice that is constantly under assault. He is protecting the goal and stopping the other team from scoring. He is the prayer warrior – the intercessor, the watchmen on the wall, determined, no matter the cost, to stop the opposing team from scoring.

Locker room: Seeing yourself or someone else waiting in a locker room speaks to release in to ministry or a work God has ordained. This could be pregame preparation or half-time encouragement. In either case, it is a call to get ready and prepare to fulfill your calling.

Monopoly: The game of Monopoly speaks to growth and expansion where God is giving you the gift of favor and expanding your sphere of influence. Monopoly is about taking territory and increasing your footprint in life.

Track: Track is a game of endurance. Paul speaks of running in a race four times in the New Testament and in each case he is using the symbolism of a race to encourage the saints to press on and run the race of faith as if to win (Acts 20:24; 1 Corinthians 9:24; 2 Timothy 4:7; Hebrews 4:7). The key elements are to run with endurance, to finish the course, and to win.

Stage, Platforms

Seeing a stage, platform, auditorium, audience, curtain call, or podium points to preparation for the next season in your life. God is setting the stage and getting ready to release you into a new area of ministry. He is orchestrating things in such a way to release you into new measures of favor. When the stage is set and you hear the curtain call, it's time to enter into your destiny and calling in the Lord.

Chapter 15

T-Z

Tickets

Tickets are interesting symbols. There are so many types of tickets: Winning tickets, "two tickets to paradise" (Eddie Money), "Ticket to Ride" (the Beatles), Golden ticket (Charlie and the Chocolate Factory), speeding ticket, tickets of admission, ticket book, and so on. Like always, context will tell the tale. The following demonstrate the possible meaning of various tickets:

Golden Ticket: Financial provision. God is restoring all the years the locusts have eaten and bringing you to a place of prosperity.

Tickets to paradise and ticket books: If you see yourself handing out free tickets this can often mean the gift of evangelism, and God if give you anointed grace to give the gift of salvation to the lost.

Ticket to ride and tickets of admission: This is all about transition and destiny. A ticket to access a train, for example, may mean the God is opening doors and taking you into a new place in Him or new areas of ministry. If the destiny is to a specific location, say, "China," the Lord is opening doors for work or intersession for that nation. A ticket to ride a Farris wheel, for example, can mean God is calling you to relaxation and life balance. If wants you to enjoy the ride with Him, and learn to live with Joy in your heart.

Tickets of warning: If you receive a ticket from a police officer for a traffic violation this is a godly warning regarding your walk with Him. You are violating His will in some aspect of your life. A speeding ticket is a call to slow down and access your direction. Running a stop sign can mean that you are doing something and God wants you to stop. Failing to yield in traffic could be attitudinal, and God is calling you to love and yield to your neighbor, to be cognizant of your fellow man and give precedence to others before yourself. In all cases, there is a call to change, either your heart or direction.

Winning tickets: At the heart of a winning ticket is the fulfillment of a dream, it carries the weight of surprise. Dreams, visions, quests that may appear to have dissipated, and the Lord is saying, "You win, this dream is for you." Winning tickets can also me prayers of provision answered. God cares about your provisional needs.

Time

Symbolism involving time include calendars, clocks, hour-glass, seasons, sunsets, sunrise, high noon, and night. Each speaking to change, wither it's in the current season or its pointing to the next season of your life. God is always on time. He is never late and is always calling us to that next level in our walk with Him. Sometimes we are under time constraints.

Other times God is setting up a divine appointment. He is using this symbolism to point the way. In either case, time is on our side and God is the one who opens and no man can shut and who closes, and no man can open. Sometimes He is restoring hope and reminding you of your destiny in Him. Remember, in Christ, it is always your time.

Tools

"Therefore whoever hears these sayings of Mine, and does them, I will liken him to a wise man who built his house on the rock: and the rain descended, the floods came, and the winds blew and beat on that house; and it did not fall, for it was founded on the rock.

But everyone who hears these sayings of Mine, and does not do them, will be like a foolish man who built his house on the sand: and the rain descended, the floods came, and the winds blew and beat on that house; and it fell. And great was its fall."

- Matthew 7:24-28

Scenes involving tools or construction are very interesting.

Tools are used to fix or repair something and secondly, to build or construct something. The Holy Spirit is so vested in your life and destiny in Christ that He is constantly working to hone your life into the image of Christ. This honing process involves not just your character, but also your mind, will, and emotions. He is vested in renewing the whole person, body, soul, and spirit of a person. The symbolism of tools (various kinds) can point to this type of work in your life, for example:

Ax: An ax is used to clear a path, to create fuel for fire (wood), or to chip away at a root system. The cutting way of brush or trees can speak to expansion of your territory or clearing a path in the direction the Lord is taking you. Chopping wood speaks to being filled with the Holy Spirit and gathering the fuel needed to sustain you in your life. An ax laid to the root of a tree speaks to areas of healing and removing negative root systems in your life. Many times situations, sins, and mindsets of our past can create a root system. Unless the ax is laid to the root of that tree, a stronghold in that area of our lives will drive us. The ax becomes a sozo moment where the Holy Spirit moves us in the process of setting us free from bondage or ways of thinking.

Chisel: A chisel is symbolic of one of two things. The first is that of chipping away as in sculpting or carving. This is the process of transformation and being conformed into the image of Christ. The second is engraving, where God is chiseling His word for you into your heart. This can be a life mission or a truth of scripture embedded in your spirit.

Hammer: Jeremiah (23:29) compares the Word of God to a hammer. A hammer has the power to construct areas in our life together. This nailing together is symbolized in the nailing of Himself to the cross. It is here, in that place, that all of our sins have been covered and dealt with. When you see, for example, a carpenter securing the framework of a house to a foundation, this may refer to God building your core belief system with the power and truth of His word. Kingdom infrastructure is what will sustain you in your life-walk with Christ.

Monkey Wrench: Seeing imagery such as a leaky faucet being repaired may point to areas in your life that are stopping the flow of the Holy Spirit and need healed, refreshed, or filled. This can be a call to rest or it may point to areas of a lack of trust. When we get tired or worn, we lose our ability to function in the Spirit. We constantly need the sweet presence of the Lord to fill us, and to rest in His nature and love for us. Dependency on Him and in Him will keep the water flowing.

Plane: Scenes such as a carpenter planning a piece of wood often speaks to striping away an area of your life. This is about preparation. God is smoothing out the surface of your life and preparing you for the next level.

Saw: Saws speak to a cutting away of something. This again is construction. The care and vestment of the carpenter creates the measure of a man. There is an old carpenter saying, Measure twice – cut once. God is in the business of constructing you. He is all about precision.

Transportation

Vehicles such as bikes, cars, trucks, boats, planes, and trains often speak of your ministry. The vehicle type can speak to the size, scope, or condition of your ministry. The Holy Spirit is very creative in this regard. I remember the Lord showing me farmers ridding wave-runners on the ocean. They were in formation riding the wave of His presence. I was struck by the parallelism of the wave runners to the fore runners of evangelism (i.e. John the Baptist).

This generation of believers, was revivalists bringing the power of the Spirit to a new generation and ushering in renewal as they rode the wave of His presence. This was a harvest move in the power of the Holy Spirit.

Other areas of transportation involve the condition of the vehicle. On the other hand, how the vehicle is being stored is important. Here are a few examples.

Car Crash: This is symbolic of a warning regarding your walk in ministry. This can also refer to something that hurt you in this regard. Did you hit someone due to driving too fast? If so, it's time to slow down and regain your bearings. Where you rear-ended? If so, this can be because of warfare or being hurt by someone.

Cracked Windshield: A cracked windshield also speaks to impaired vision, however, often this refers to something that hurt you in your past and the residue of that wound is hindering how you view thing. Like seeing through rose-colored glasses, your vision is filtered and God wants to bring healing to that area of your life.

Flat Tire: Symbolic of being stuck or the inability to get where you are trying to go. A flat tire is a tire with a leak. All the air that enabled it to move is gone. Air is symbolic of the Holy Spirit and the loss of air speaks to the need to be filled and refreshed.

Garage or Carport: Seeing a car parked in a garage or under a carport speaks two one of two things: 1. Covering – this symbolizes the order of the kingdom and the power of being in the right relationship in the body and under authority. 2. Rest and being hidden in Christ – this symbolizes a season of rest and rejuvenation where God hides you in the palm of His hand and uses this season to speak life under the safety and shelter of His wings. This is a season of reflection and honoring who God is for you. It is important to remember all the wondrous things He has done. It is a time of strengthening your inner man to run the next leg of the race.

Out of Gas: Running out of gas is symbolic of running out of energy and the need to be refreshed and filled with the Holy Spirit. This is a call to rest. A balanced life and continuous filling of the Holy Spirit is the only thing that will sustain your ministry.

Stolen Vehicle: Experiencing a robbery where your vehicle is stolen or someone is trying to take it from you symbolizes an act of warfare where the enemy of your soul is trying to rob you of your destiny. This is a demonic assault to stop you from attaining all that God has for you. God uses this symbolism to awaken you to a warfare stance and to stand firm and use your authority in Christ to rebuke the enemy and press in.

Vehicle Fishtailing: Fishtailing is symbolic of being out of control or feeling out of control.

Vehicle Restoration: Seeing a vehicle being restored or seeing a restored antique car can speak to two things:

1. Revitalized call late in life. When the promises of God seem to tarry and you find yourself thinking of dreams that have never been fulfilled, God is igniting dreams from your past and calling you into your destiny. He is restoring the years the locusts have eaten and bringing your life mission or dream to reality. Remember you are never too old to dream and walk in your destiny.

2. Restoration of a past anointing or an incomplete work from the past. The ministry of the past is our heritage and they become our floor so we can take it to the next level.

Windshield Wipers: Dirty windows or a windshield that is being hammered by rain speaks to an inability to see clearly. This can be a result of an issue in your life or the result of warfare being waged against you. Wipers washing away the debris speak to the Holy Spirit bringing clarity of vision and guiding you in the midst of the storm.

Trees

Trees are amazing. The Lord's use of trees as symbols of His Word a will are so abundant it is mind-boggling. Genesis opens with the story of two trees: the "tree of life" and the "tree of the knowledge of good and evil." The book of Revelation closes with the "tree of life" as an emblem of the joys of the celestial paradise. Moses was drawn to his destiny by seeing the manifestation of God's presence in a burning Acacia tree that was not consumed.

Peter refers to Christ on the cross as "who Himself bore our sins in His own body on the tree, that we, having died to sins, might live for righteousness—by whose stripes you were healed (1 Peter 2:24; see Acts 5:30, 10:39, 13:29)."

Of course, Jesus utilizes trees as a metaphor throughout the gospels. We see the character of man defined by a tree and its fruit:

> *"Even so, every good tree bears good fruit, but a bad tree bears bad fruit. A good tree cannot bear bad fruit, nor can a bad tree bear good fruit. Every tree that does not bear good fruit is cut down and thrown into the fire. Therefore by their fruits you will know them."*
>
> *- Matthew 7:17-20*

The Kingdom of Heaven and its influence upon the planet is described as a tree:

> *"The kingdom of heaven is like a mustard seed, which a man took and sowed in his field, which indeed is the least of all the seeds; but when it is grown it is greater than the herbs and becomes a tree, so that the birds of the air come and nest in its branches*

- Matthew 13:31-32

The fruit of Israel is re-erred to as a withering fig tree (Matthew 21:18-21). The timetable of Christ's return is hidden in the parable of the fig tree (Matthew 24:32).

Paul uses the symbol of a wild olive tree to explain how gentile believers were grafted into the body of Christ. Jesus, himself is referred to as the Branch (Isaiah 11:1, Zechariah 3:6-8). In John 15, Jesus referred to us as branches and He as the vine, when speaking about our necessity to abide in Him. We also see in Zechariah 4, two "olive trees" flowing with the oil of anointing continually to the lampstand (His body the Church). Finely, David refers to God's children as "Trees of the Lord" Psalm 104:16, a fruitful tree in Psalm 1:3, a "green olive tree" Psalm 52:8, and a "palm tree" in Psalm 92:12.

The Lord has used trees to speak to me in so many ways it is amazing. In a dream He called me to the high place of His presence as I watched myself scaling a might pine tree. I saw the wind of the Spirit blowing between the leaves of a weeping willow during a season of transition. I heard the Lord speak of healing as I watched the bark of a birch tree peel away exposing the white inner wood. I saw the angels of God standing at attention as mighty red woods I ascended to the top of a mountain. I watched creation groan for the revealing of the Sons of God as I saw trees weeping tears of sap. Trees are powerful in the language of God. Let's look at a few trees and their possible meaning.

Acacia Tree: There are a number of acacia trees mentioned in the scripture, the most notable being Moses's burning bush. A common variety of acacia is the thorny acacia tree. This was probably the tree that Moses had seen. It's interesting to note that some scholars believe that the crown of thorns that was placed on the head of Jesus was made from the thorny acacia.

Many of the articles in the tabernacle were made of acacia wood. Acacia wood was also used to make incense (henna). Seeing a thorny acacia tree may point to worship and redemption, pointing you to praise Him and His redemptive work in your life.

Almond Tree: Almond trees are often a symbol of God's promise to perform His word (Jeremiah 1:11, Genesis 43:11). They can also speak to anointing and confirmation as in Aaron's rod. Sometimes it can mean watchfulness and to be awake (Jeremiah 1:12). Other times it may refer to your place in the body and His anointing over your life as in the Candlestick of Exodus 25:31-39.

Apple Tree: Apple trees often speak of God's love for you (Psalm 17:8) or the love of a married couple (Song of Solomon 2:5, 7:8). It's interesting the David's "*Apple of the Eye*" latterly means the "Gate of the Eye" which may speak to a release of the prophetic and the seer's gift (Zechariah 2:8).

Bark: Bark can speak of several things. First, it can symbolize the flesh and a striping away of those things that are not pleasing to the Lord. Secondly, it may symbolize strength as in the shield of faith that protects your spiritual vital organs.

Branch: Speaks to abiding in Christ and your place in the body or network of believers.

Eucalyptus Tree: As a native Californian Eucalyptus, trees were a major part of the landscape in my life. Whenever I travel back to California, I am drawn into memories of my childhood sparked by the aroma and beauty of these smooth majestic trees. One of the by-products of this tree is its oil, steam distilled to create sweets, cough drops, decongestants, and toothpaste. Seeing this tree may peak to the promise of healing or the fragrance of His life in you to touch others and bring refreshing and healing to others.

Fig Tree: The fig tree is the third tree mentioned by name in the Bible, after the Tree of the knowledge of good and evil, and the Tree of Life. In Deuteronomy, the Promised Land is describe as,

> *"A land of wheat and barley, of vines and fig trees and pomegranates, a land of olive oil and honey; a land in which you will eat bread without scarcity, in which you will lack nothing; a land whose stones are iron and out of whose hills you can dig copper"*
>
> \- Deuteronomy 8:8-10

Proverbs uses the tending of the fig tree as a symbol of caring of the Master's needs (Proverbs 27:18). Ironically, the fig is the only tree pollinated by the wasp speaking to the reward obtained after seasons of struggle and adversity. The fruit is sweet, rich, and costly. Its aroma is inescapable.

As a child, I lived next to a fig orchard surrounded by eucalyptus trees and the combined aroma was amazing. When figs are ripe, the skin often bursts weeping out sweet nectar. Seeing figs speaks to rich fruitfulness in your life and the favor and blessings of God upon your life. The fig is a sign of honor and your place in the Kingdom (Proverbs 27:18).

Forest: Seeing a forest often speaks to the nations or navigation the public sphere. If the focus is on a trail in the woods, it may symbolize a current season in your life and point to navigation during this time of walking with God. Seeing a forest fire can symbolize trouble or calamity coming upon the nations. Seeing a forest ranger symbolizes the Holy Spirit as the helper in times of need.

Log: Logs can symbolize a couple things. If the context is gathering firewood, then the meaning may point to the need to refuel with the in filling of the Holy Spirit in seasons of isolation. If a log is being plucked from a fire this points to the glory of redemption and the saving grace of Christ. If the log is stripped down and transformed into usable wood for construction, this symbolizes the work of God in your life to transform you into His image.

Oak Tree: Oaks often speak to strength but more specifically your ability to endure and persevere during extreme seasons in your life (Isaiah 6:3; Ezekiel 6:13).

Olive Tree: Olive trees are wonderful. They often speak to the endless supply of the anointing oil of God (Zechariah 4). The also speak to the fruitfulness in your life and symbolize your union with Christ in the Kingdom of God (Romans 11:17). An olive tree may also symbolize end times evangelism and power in the Holy Spirit (Revelation 11:4). A green olive tree speaks to a prosperous Christian (Psalm 52:8).

Palm Tree: A palm tree is symbolic of the peace of Christ in your life (Song of Solomon 7:8), or prosperity and blessing in your life (Psalm 92:12; Exodus 15:27). They can also symbolize worship and honor of Christ the King (John 12:13; Revelation 7:9).

Pine Trees: I love pine trees. The evergreen aroma calls me to press in to the wonders of God. Their tall majestic nature adorns mountainous regions around the world. Pine trees are strong and armored with thick scaly bark. Their buds shoot out at the tips and their fruit (the pinecone) produces both male and female cones. The seeds of the pine are small and flavorful (pine nuts and pesto).

However, the seeds are only released when a bird breaks open the cone with its beak. However, some cones may release their seeds on their own, but only after a number of years. Pine trees grow in acidic soil and, like us, need fire to regenerate. This is symbolic of the fire of the Holy Spirit. Their leaves are needle like, strong, and piercing. Their aroma can transform the atmosphere of a room (potpourri). Pine trees point to Christ's birth as seen in the living room of every Christian at Christmas. Pines speak to you in your full strength and destiny in the Lord. They call out to you and point to your potential. Pine trees are an invention to climb higher and speak to the power of endurance and legacy. Pines speak to the glory of God in your life.

Sap: Sap is the lifeblood of all plants. The water-based fluid brings nutrients from the root system to all extremities. Seeing trees weeping sap can symbolize many things from the blood of Christ to the tears of creation calling all Saints to fulfill their destiny. Psalm 104:16 proclaim, "*The trees of the Lord are full of sap....*" The fullness speaks to the life-blood of our Savior and calls for the abundance of His saving grace.

Stump: Seeing a stump speaks of judgment (Daniel 4:15-26), but with the judgment is the promise of redemption. In Nebuchadnezzar's pride, judgment was pronounced, but only for a season. After repentance is sanity returned and freedom was realized (Job 14:8).

> *"Though its root may grow old in the earth, and its stump may die in the ground, yet at the scent of water it will bud and bring forth branches like a plant."*

Repentance always brings forth life; sin on the other hand brings forth death.

Sycamore: Seeing a sycamore tree typically speaks to being called out for service by the Lord. The prophet Amos said, "*I was no prophet, nor was I a son of a prophet, but I was a sheep breeder and a tender of sycamore fruit. Then the Lord took me as I followed the flock, and the Lord said to me, go, prophesy to My people Israel.*" The most famous story of one being called out is Zacchaeus in the book of Luke. In this story, Zacchaeus is so eager to see Jesus that he climbs a sycamore tree to get a better view. When Jesus saw him He said, (Luke 19:5)

> *"Zacchaeus, make haste and come down, for today I must stay at your house."*

With eagerness and joy, he came down from that tree, went to Jesus, and offered to give half his goods to the poor. Jesus response was (Luke 19:8),

> *"Today salvation has come to this house, because he also is a son of Abraham; 10 for the Son of Man has come to seek and to save that which was lost."*

The symbol of the sycamore can be either a call to salvation or a call to witness to the lost or to the prophetic ministry.

Weeping Willow: Weeping willows speak of a season of sorrow and the promise of hope and comfort. The promise of God found in Psalms 23:4-5 is this,

> *"Yea, though I walk through the valley of the shadow of death, I will fear no evil; for You are with me; Your rod and Your staff, they comfort me. You prepare a table before me in the presence of my enemies; You anoint my head with oil; My cup runs over."*

Bibliography

Jim Driscoll, The Modern Seer, 2010, Orbital Book Group, 1st Ed.

Doug Addison, Prophecy, Dreams, and Evangelism, 2005, Streams Books, 1st Ed.

Kris Vallotton, Developing a Supernatural Lifestyle, 2007, Destiny Image, 1st Ed.

Jonathan Welton, The School of the Seer, 2009, Destiny Image, 1st Ed.

Dr. Bill Hamon, Apostles, Prophets, and the Coming Moves of God, 1997, Destiny Image, 1st Ed.

Graham Cooke, Approaching the Heart of Prophecy, 2009, Brilliant Books, 1st Ed.; Developing Your Prophetic Gifting, 1994, Chosen Books, 1st Ed.

About the Author

Fred Raynaud, CEC, CCA – is an Author, speaker, and Chef by trade. He serves as the Founder and President of CELI (Culinary Executive Leadership Institute) and the Founder of the Dreamweaver Outreach program, a street ministry bringing God's touch to the streets.

For more information, please visit our website at
http://www.SeersGift.com